Hollywood Movies on the Couch

*A Psychoanalyst
Examines 15 Famous Films*

Hollywood Movies on the Couch

A Psychoanalyst
Examines 15 Famous Films

by Henry Kellerman

BARRICADE
BOOKS

Published by Barricade Books Inc.
185 Bridge Plaza North
Suite 309
Fort Lee, N.J. 07024
www.barricadebooks.com

ISBN: 978-1-56980-459-9

Library of Congress Cataloging-in-Publication Data

Kellerman, Henry. : Hollywood on the couch / by Henry Kellerman.
    p. cm.
 ISBN: 978-1-56980-459-9
1. Psychoanalysis in motion pictures. 2. Psychoanalysis and motion
pictures. I. Title.
 PN1995.9.P783K45 2011
 791.43'75--dc23

                                              2011049760

10 9 8 7 6 5 4 3 2 1

Manufactured in the United States of America

for

Gerald Yagoda, Ph.D.

My Jerry.

From Kings County (and Lisa), through Middletown (and Florence), to the East End of Long Island.

The journey was great and you always did it first.

and for

Marsha Yagoda

Beautiful Marsha.

They were the best hamburgers.

BOOKS BY THE AUTHOR

Authored Books
The Psychoanalysis of Symptoms
Dictionary of Psychopathology
Group Psychotherapy and Personality: Intersecting Structures
Sleep Disorders: Insomnia and Narcolepsy
The 4 Steps to Peace of Mind: The Simple Effective Way to Cure Our Emotional Symptoms. (Romanian edition, 2008; Japanese edition, 2011)
Love Is Not Enough: What It Takes to Make It Work
Haggadah: A Passover Seder for the Rest of Us
Greedy, Cowardly, and Weak: Hollywood's Jewish Stereotypes
Hollywood Movies on the Couch: A Psychoanalyst Examines 15 Famous Films
Personality: How it Forms
The Discovery of God: A Psycho/Evolutionary Perspective
The Making of Ghosts (A Novel)

Co-authored Books
(with Anthony Burry, Ph.D.)
Psychopathology and Differential Diagnosis: A Primer
Volume 1: History of Psychopathology
Volume 2: Diagnostic Primer
Handbook of Psychodiagnostic Testing: Analysis of Personality in the Psychological Report. 1st edition; 1981; 2nd edition, 1991; 3rd edition; 1997; 4th edition, 2007. (Japanese edition, 2011).

Edited Books
Group Cohesion: Theoretical and Clinical Perspectives
The Nightmare: Psychological and Biological Foundations

Co-edited Books
(with Robert Plutchik, Ph.D.)
Emotion: Theory, Research, and Experience
Volume 1: Theories of Emotion
Volume 2: Emotions in Early Development
Volume 3: Biological Foundations of Emotion
Volume 4: The Measurement of Emotion
Volume 5: Emotion, Psychopathology, and Psychotherapy

TABLE OF CONTENTS

Part 1: SOLOS

Part 2: DUETS

Part 3: TRIOS

INTRODUCTION

This book is about psychoanalyzing movies. More specifically, one key character (or in some cases, the writer-director) from each selected film will lie on the psychoanalytic couch, and you will either listen in on their session, or simply be privy to the analyst's narrative of the case. The aim here is to discover underlying meaning to a character's personality and motivation through a psychoanalytic excavation.

Of course, movies have the power to touch emotions — emotions that want to be touched. In that dark theatre we become completely vicarious — as though what's happening on the screen is happening to us, even though, of course, we know it's not. At its best, the experience of watching film is different from a voyeuristic excursion; it can actually be cathartic, perhaps, even as art implicitly promises, it can be curative.

A work of art, some people will tell you, can help set you free. Being absorbed by the story therefore, is frequently an opportunity to grow emotionally, and in that way the whole viewing experience can help in the working out of some psychological issue of one's life. And that actually happens sometimes.

Basically, the problem in which a character in the movie is engaged reveals a struggle — and how the story unfolds allows us to see that such a struggle is important and valuable. In this way, we too, are invited into the importance of struggle in our own lives.

In this sense, a well crafted story has the power to confirm one's internal narrative—how you see yourself. This is what we loved about stories when we were children. They touched things deep within us: our needs, our fears, our angers, our desires, our dissatisfactions, and our hopes. So when we go to the movies, the films become our stories—all kinds of stories, that because of Hollywood, are at our fingertips; just pay the price, get the ticket, sit and watch the screen—the beautiful, hopeful screen that offers us the opportunity to be swept away.

Acknowledgements

For his thoughtful and conscientious edit of this book, I would like to express my sincere appreciation to my son, Max Kellerman. It was he who suggested I write this book, the first time I had ever undertaken the task of writing a book based on someone else's vision. Yet, because I had already published a book titled *Greedy, Cowardly, and Weak: Hollywood's Jewish Stereotypes*, it seemed like a good idea to also consider the subject matter of this present book.

When I finished a first draft of this book, Max then engaged the manuscript both with a circumspect attitude, as well as with an iron-fisted grip on keeping the basic spine of each chapter strong and straight, of course, minus discursive unnecessary tangents.

I owe Max many thanks for the enormous time, effort, and focus that he, with grace and heart, gave to the project.

A special thank you has been dearly earned by my publisher, Carole Stuart, who with remarkable skill and know-how also contributed a variety of very useful comments and suggestions throughout the publication process. And to Suzanne Henry, I extend a very grateful thank you for her astute copyediting.

Apart from my life-long interest in movies, I thought that my work as a psychoanalyst would enable me to enter the world of movie story-telling from an interesting vantage point, so I fixed on a number of films about which I had already entertained certain psychological insights. This newer perspective seemed also to shed a different light on the meaning of the particular story of these films.

The Format of the Book

The book is divided into three parts with each part containing the examination of five films. The films in all three parts of the book represent releases of movies sampling each decade from the 1940's through the first decade of the 21st century.

Part 1: Solos

In the first part of the book I have selected five films in which a main character of the story goes it alone and we see how a single person experiences, manages to cope with, and expresses personal issues.

Chapter 1
The Conversation (1974)

Chapter 2
The Day of the Jackal (1973)

Chapter 3
Predator (1987)

Chapter 4
Superheroes (1978, 1989, 2002)

Chapter 5
The Passion of the Christ (2004)

PART 2: DUETS

In the second part of the book I look at five films in which two characters need to work out their problem(s) as a dyad, together, even though only one of the couple will be the person analyzed—the pivotal one.

Chapter 6
When Harry Met Sally (1989)

Chapter 7
Husbands and Wives (1992)

Chapter 8
The Bridge on the River Kwai (1957)

Chapter 9
Pretty Woman (1990)

Chapter 10
The Way We Were (1973)

PART 3: TRIOS

In the third part of the book we will consider films in which problems are created because of the crowded nature when there are three in a relationship; one of the three will be the key person on the couch.

Chapter 11
Casablanca (1942)

Chapter 12
The Graduate (1967)

Chapter 13
The Ghost and Mrs. Muir (1947)

Chapter 14
Laura (1944)

Chapter 15
The Birds (1963)

SUMMARY

In the *Summary* of the book, the essential psychological issue of each part of the book is encapsulated. This will be done by aiming the magnifying glass at the motivation of characters designated as to whether they were, more or less acting it alone as in Part 1: **Solos,** or as a member of a couple, as in Part 2: **Duets**, or in a crowded threesome as in Part 3: **Trios**.
Now, to Part 1: **Solos**.

PART 1

SOLOS

PART 1

SOLOS

Chapter 1

THE CONVERSATION
(Released, 1974)

Co-producer: Fred Roos
Associate producer: Mona Skager
Original Music by David Shire
Written, Produced, and Directed by
Francis Ford Coppola

Main Cast

Gene Hackman	Harry Caul
John Cazale	Stan
Allen Garfield	William P. 'Bernie' Moran
Frederic Forrest	Mark
Cindy Williams	Ann
Terri Garr	Amy Fredericks
Harrison Ford	Martin Stett
Elizabeth MacRae	Meredith
Michael Higgins	Paul
Phoebe Alexander	Lurleen

Sample Supporting Cast

Robert Duvall	The Director
Mark Wheeler	Receptionist
Robert Shields	Mime
Gian-Carlo Coppola	Boy in church
Al Nalbandian	Salesman at Surveillance Convention
Billy Dee Williams	Man in Yellow Hat

Introduction

It's the 1970's, an era of privacy concerns, and post-Kennedy conspiracy theories that people can feel in their bones. It's just about the time of post-Watergate and all the eavesdropping and double-dealing delinquencies, and flat-out illegalities of the Nixon years. Fitting right into the time and theme of paranoia, we get Coppola's *The Conversation,* a surveillance-genre film in a category pre and post *The Conversation* that includes: Michelangelo Antonioni's *Blow Up*; Tony Scott's *Enemy of the State*; The *Bourne* films of Doug Liman/Paul Greengrass; Brian De Palma's *Blow Out*; Irwin Winkler's *The Net*; and, even Hitchcock's *Rear Window*.

The Issue of Privacy

The issue is privacy violation: a power discrepancy between those who spy on you for advantage, and who therefore have the power, and those who are the targets of such vigilante behavior and who because of it, can be essentially rendered helpless, powerless. From a strictly psychoanalytic point of view it also relates to voyeurism and its compulsively urgent impulse—stalking! This is stalking behavior designed to invade your privacy in order to capture you nakedly complicit; it's an insidious assault on one's inviolability.

Coppola gives us Harry Caul (played by Gene Hackman), the ace of aces in surveillance—especially in the gadgeteer's world of the most exotic electronic audio surveillance techniques available. As much as he's the world's expert in insinuating himself through the boundaries of anyone a client hires him to snoop on, he's equally adept at not permitting anyone or anything to ever violate his own personal boundary. No one gets to Harry Caul. He's not attached to anyone—no family, no particular cultural sub-group, no favorite baseball team, nothing like that. He's not controlled by any obligation to person or agency and he is certain that he absolutely must insulate himself from any potential violation that is always and relentlessly, he believes, coming toward him.

Harry knows better than anyone—the world is wired!

Harry's growth-arc becomes a vivid contrast between how it all begins—a man doing his job without regard to implications or consequences (as Harry proclaims "I don't care what they're talking about, all I want is a nice fat recording")—and how it ends, as a man struggling with his conscience, his very being, in order to be able to do the right thing, and at the same time, possibly save himself.

The Main Story

The DVD describes the story this way:

"... [a] provoking mystery-drama explores the morality of privacy as Harry Caul, expert surveillance man ... [in] ... a routine wire-tapping job ... [finds that it] ... turns into a modern nightmare as Harry hears something disturbing in his recording of a young couple in a park. He begins to worry about what the tape may be used for, and becomes involved in a maze of secrecy and murder. . . ."

Gotcha

In what appears to be a case of simple marital infidelity, a high-powered corporate executive called "The President" (played by Robert Duvall) retains Harry to gather information about a suspected affair between his wife, Ann (played by Cindy Williams), and her presumed lover, Mark (played by Frederic Forrest). The information is to be contained in audio recordings of conversations as well as in candid photos.

It's lunch time in Union Square Park in San Francisco, crowded with people and activity. In the middle of it all, Harry is shadowing the couple by walking aimlessly among the crowd. Of course he is wired. He also has several confederates working with him. One is also walking along in the crowd well fitted with a listening device, while another is on a rooftop pointing an audio-rifle at the couple—a powerful audio gizmo that can pick up conversations even from a football field away—and still another is on a high floor in a commercial building at an open window with a radar antenna. Along with this, the mother ship is a panel truck parked nearby and manned by Harry's assistant, Stan (played by John Cazale). This panel truck is the hub of it all and is completely stacked with all sorts of recording equipment. The truck is also fitted with one-way viewing windows so that those inside the truck can see outside but if looking into the window from outside, one will only be looking into a mirror.

"I can see you but you can't see me," and "I can hear you, but you can't hear me," is the essential message and symbolic meaning of that entire particular gorgeously arranged and directed opening scene. There is even a mime in the park in white-face and costume walking around aping the expressive demeanor of people—symbolic commentary on the entire 'shadowing' surveillance theme. When Harry visits his client's, opulent office, set on the floor directly in full view, in the middle of the office, rests a powerful telescope pointed at the window and beyond. Harry naturally squints into it; Why not? It's simply a reflexive example of what he does—the nature of his voyeuristic stalking reflex.

On the surface, the story is generally about the electronic surveillance industry where they 'gotcha,' or where they're 'gonna getcha;' about how the power of technology can be used to support the power of one group over another. Specifically, it's about how Harry Caul uses this technology to separate himself from the world in the absence of any ethical or moral measure. It's a world of communication made through remote connections, through remote transmissions. Consistent with his distant and cold need for privacy, Harry has a girlfriend, Amy (played by Terri Garr), who he keeps in an apartment that he pays for. Not surprisingly, she doesn't know where Harry lives, nor does she have his phone number. In fact he denies that he even has a phone. Of course, we know better.

Harry is known throughout the surveillance industry as top gun. Everyone wants his services but Harry doesn't work for anyone else and therefore is not compelled to do anyone's bidding. He is an independent contractor who keeps professional and clients' secrets from his employees, even from Stan. Harry's suspiciousness and guardedness is obviously, world class.

Harry Caul lives alone in an apartment building. At one time he lived in New York City, but while on a surveillance job in the city, his snooping contributed to the death of three people. Harry claims it was inadvertent that his material caused those deaths and he has continued to try to convince himself that it was all indirect; that is, that there was no through-line from his work to the deadly deeds. He says it wasn't his fault, but we see that from time to time, it does in fact intrude into his consciousness, and it bothers him. His residual nagging thought is why anything about his work should continue to bother him.

So, even on a quasi-conscious level it got him, as in 'gotcha.'

Harry's apartment door has several locks installed, and an alarm goes off when the door opens. His apartment is nondescript—neutral as can be; neutral as he himself wants to be, and is. After all, in his shadowing of others, he needs to be a face in the crowd—no one. At one point he arrives home and finds that without his permission his landlady had entered his apartment. Harry is perplexed and—alarmed! It's incredible to him that she had actually gained entry to his apartment. What?! It's Harry's birthday and somehow she knew it? In other words, he's obsessed, and struck with the idea that someone gained access to him without his permission. This of course, is an invasion of his boundary, a profound violation that he cannot tolerate. In a tone that is moderate and yet direct, he telephones the landlady and in no uncertain terms tells her that entering his apartment is 'verboten.'

So, here we have it. Even his super, super-vigilance, wasn't super enough, wasn't fool-proof; apparently it didn't help seal his privacy. And this access his landlady had to his 'interior' is something that surely went against his grain, it constituted a quintessential breach of his core concern.

'Gotcha!'

Could this violation of his inviolability be a foreshadowing of things yet to come?

Harry May Not Be As Impermeable As He Thinks

Harry gradually pieces together all of the conversations his audio equipment picked up. His equipment is designed to screen out background noise and to do all sorts of fantastic pirouettes in order to actually hear conversation that would ordinarily be impossible to hear because of such background din, static, and so forth. But Harry can do it—can he ever—and in piecing it altogether, it dawns on him that a murder is being planned, presumably by his client (or, who knows?). Since Harry is suspicious about everything, then even the audience doesn't know who might be planning the murder (if indeed a murder is in fact being planned), or who might be the victim (assuming there even is a victim).

The story then takes us through all sorts of twists and turns. Harry attends a surveillance convention and is approached by people he knows, and by people who claim to know him though he doesn't recognize them. He meets a callgirl who accompanies him to a party at his own audio shop. The so-called attraction this woman has for Harry lets her slip successfully under his guard, under his protective radar. They go to bed, and while Harry is sleeping, she steals the tapes.

Unbeknownst to him, Harry has already been taped by another surveillance specialist, the east coast top-gun in the business, Bernie Moran (played by Allen Garfield). This, along with how he was deceived by the woman who stole his tapes, and by his landlady gaining access to his apartment, comprises three instances where Harry Caul was bested because implicitly, and against his will, his privacy was breached.

'Gotcha!'

Harry begins to feel that he's no longer impenetrable. Apparently, he cannot prevent this migration of foreign elements into his soul, into his heart of hearts. Some of this foreign stuff is viral, and out to do him in. But other of this foreign stuff is per chance a new-found conscience and newly cohering (but not yet fully cohered) self. And because it might be new, it's also not completely comfortable. To top it off, it must be confusing to him to have two disparate foreign or new elements inundating him simultaneously. And both elements feel dangerous because one can tangibly hurt him physically (those now monitoring him), while the other (a conscience) can threaten the psychological defenses of his personality that he's spent a lifetime building—that intangible stuff.

Before he began to gestate this conscience, Harry would always answer "No" to any request for togetherness: to wit, his former girlfriend's request for togetherness, or as another example, when Bernie Moran asks him to join in a partnership and without skipping a beat Harry directly says: "I don't need anyone!"

But, we may ask: What about the possible new Harry Caul? Does he not need anyone?

Harry Caul on the Couch

In psychological terms, Harry is an encapsulated paranoid character who is not psychotic but rather is entirely radiated with a personality-paranoia characterized by suspicious and guarded behavior patterns, as well as reacting with a some-what schizoid inclination (feeling and remaining distant from others). And in this entirely independent, autonomous and pro-phylactic precautionary state, Harry Caul starts his journey in a solo role; in a sense he is starting at the zero point—alone.

Thus, the challenge Coppola sets for Harry concerns choic-es: 1) he can stay at that zero point throughout the story; 2) he can become contaminated (decline further) which would give him some extent of a minus zero score; or, 3) he can begin to gradually feel feelings (even some empathy), so that he can begin to gain a moral ascendancy which would put him into some extent of a zero plus score.

Harry does have a gradual upsurge of conscience regard-ing his job and what it entails; how gathering information in a so-called subliminal fashion can profoundly negatively affect the object of the investigation—that is to say, negatively af-fect the person being investigated. He even tries confession at church where he attempts to cleanse himself of the refuse that this emerging new probing conscience wants expelled from his soul.

Harry's growth can be seen because his paranoia that was a constant lurking presence of suspicion and distrust, and that fortified his schizoid aloof and distant stance, is now being challenged by an existential confrontation with this newly, yet tentatively probing conscience.

Harry Caul—A Solo Performer

As a solo performer, Harry's is a story of a person with inner demons and how they impact his relationship with him-self. It is the factor that places this story in the category of

Solos. In the past Harry's general paranoia, and more specifically, his guardedness, wouldn't let anything in. His defense was geared to seeing everything wrong 'out there,' and nothing wrong within. He is now apparently plagued with the sense that the reason everything would always be wrong in the world and nothing wrong with him was that he was unconsciously and monumentally worried that really, everything was wrong with him—within. Therefore, before this growing moral metamorphosis of his materialized, Harry's former typical, automatic, reflexive and unconscious decision was always to detach from feelings about the world and remain cloistered—remain alone.

Harry's Growth-Arc

It's all coming together: Harry Caul's personality, designed to be separate and isolated, along with his conscience-free applied work that existed in the absence of assessing the merits of the job of surveillance, has now entered a black hole out of which these schizoid/paranoid character patterns of his can no longer freely escape into his personality as they once did. These character patterns may no longer be able to control him. So, rather than getting pinned to the ground by the gravity of such character patterns, he has now possibly gained the ascendancy and is possibly on top of them—just possibly.

It happened gradually as Harry began lowering his guard. Then things began to change. His girlfriend left him, the other woman got close to him and poof, the tapes were gone. And at the same time that these were anxiety producing events, they were also portents of the birth of an ongoing underlying positive process.

Harry had never trusted human nature because he under-stood it his way, idiosyncratically. This meant that he could act in the absence of respect for the inviolability of others. All those locks on his apartment door were protection because of his belief that people might want to invade his privacy, invade his membrane. However, the reverse was actually closer to the truth; it was Harry's own desire to invade the privacy of others. This kind of paranoia can be expressed as an aphorism: "If you spot it, you got it." This means that nefarious motives he attrib-uted to others (which is why he needed separation from them) is in reality the reverse; it's really his own nefarious motives toward others that he kept repressed and out of his awareness. It was his very own passion and virtuosity of snooping and surveillance that was the psychological defense mechanism known as 'projection'—you attribute something to the outside that is really about you—and therefore it's not that your basic intention is to snoop on them; rather, it's your absolute belief that it's their intention to snoop on you!

But now, part of his growth arc is this advent of a new psy-chological orientation—one that possibly could mean that Harry, paradoxically, is now more alone than ever. This is so because, despite his new membership in the human race, he has lost the only person he ever really knew—himself.

Now, Harry Caul has to find a new "me."

The Raincoat

Let's go back a step or two. You see, throughout the movie Harry wears a transparent plastic raincoat even though wear-ing it has nothing whatsoever to do with rain. What is that all about? It's a prop in the movie that has been also noticed by others. Peter Cowie, in his book on Coppola, titled *Coppola*, says the raincoat represents the amniotic shroud that shields the newborn. As it turns out, this transparent raincoat is another genius Coppola symbol that captures Harry's key personality organization.

Let's start out with a bang! That transparent raincoat is a condom. It says, "I won't touch anyone, and no one can touch me." It means, "I will not have a relationship!" It's Harry's consistent display of a symbol exemplifying his isolation. The raincoat represents his refusal to let anything touch him—meaning permanent relationships. It's really an equivalent germ-phobia; that he must prevent all germs (people with nefarious motives toward him) from achieving their goal. And it is precisely this goal that Harry understands all too well because it is exactly what he's always aiming for in the getting-to-others that he does for a living.

In addition, to augment Peter Cowie's take on the raincoat, the surname Caul is defined as a covering; that is, it's the inner fetal membrane of higher vertebrates especially when covering the head at birth—the operative phrase being "covering the head."

Back on the case, Harry's expertise leads him to conclude that a murder actually took place. The perpetrators of the actual killing know that Harry has figured out what happened, and he is warned in a telephone call that they're listening to him. The tables have turned and now Harry Caul is the object of control by those whose power, like his lies, in—surveillance. He feels he's in danger because of it, and consequently feels somewhat helpless. Harry knows that now 'they' have the power.

In a frenzy, Harry tears his apartment to pieces (including prying up the floor boards and shredding the wallpaper off the walls). The entire demolished apartment looks like part of a derelict ramshackle building. He's trying, in vain, to find the listening devices. In the process he takes his religious icon figurine, one of only two prized possessions, and smashes it to smithereens thinking that it may be holding a bug. Nothing inside! It's another symbol of Harry's penumbra — how he's now living on the edge of a shadow.

Next, the raincoat is gone. He's no longer covered by it. He's now feeling covered by an inverted condition; that is, now he's the one being shadowed, watched, listened in on — controlled.

Harry is left sitting on a chair playing his saxophone. The saxophone is all that is left of him, because in dismantling and essentially wrecking the apartment he was also deconstructing himself in order to try to rescue himself. But he never checks the saxophone (his only remaining self-reference) as possibly housing some sort of listening device because it would be akin to actually suspecting himself.

We finally see Harry in a stunning final scene that is as staggering as the opening scene of the movie was beautiful. He is playing a lonely saxophone in a wasteland. At the end, raincoat or not, the message is that the struggle between being alone and not being alone is a never-ending one, and, stripped of his raincoat, his shield from the world, he's now a different person. He starts out on this new phase of his life, alone, in a deconstructed apartment — a symbol of who he was, or is.

With respect to Harry's emotional life, the gradually accelerating development of his conscience apparently did not lead to a descent into madness. Rather, more hopefully, it looks as though if Harry can reassemble himself and say goodbye to his deconstructed apartment (self), then at last he will have gained that hoped-for ascendancy.

So, the moral of the story is that in order to find yourself it looks as though you need to relinquish those trusty, life-long defenses on which you always depended.

C'mon Harry, we're rootn' for ya.

P.S. From a contemporary perspective, this film may seem dated; surveillance is of course now more sophisticated than it was three to four decades ago. Yet the story is as compelling today as it was when initially released in 1974; that is to say that it doesn't matter *how* Big Brother is watching; he *is* watching!

Chapter 2

THE DAY OF THE JACKAL
(Released, 1973)

From the novel, *The Day of the Jackal,* by Frederick Forsyth
Screenplay by Kenneth Ross
Produced by John Woolf
Co-produced by David Deutsch / Julien Derode
Original Music by Georges Delerue
Directed by Fred Zinnemann

Main Cast

Edward Fox	The Jackal
Terence Alexander	Lloyd
Michel Auclair	Colonel Rolland
Alan Badel	The Minister
Tony Britton	Inspector Thomas
Denis Carey	Casson
Adrien Cayla-Legrand	The President
Cyril Cusack	The Gunsmith
Maurice Denham	General Colbert
Vernon Dobtcheff	The Interrogator
Jacques Francois	Pascal

Olga Georges-Picot	Denise
Raymond Gerome	Flavigny
Barrie Ingham	St. Clair
Derek Jacobi	Caron
Michael Lonsdale	Lebel
Jean Martin	Wolenski
Ronald Pickup	The Forger
Eric Porter	Colonel Rodin
Delphine Seyrig	Madame Colette de Montpellier
Donald Sinden	Mallinson

Sample Supporting Cast

Anton Rodgers	Bernard
Jean Sorel	Bastien-Thiry
David Swift	Montclair
Timothy West	Berthier
Philippe Leotard	Gendarme
Edward Hardwicke	Charles Calthrop

Introduction

An assassin for hire is notorious for his cold-blooded pursuit of his prey and goes about it with impunity because no one knows him. He changes his persona, his name, his very essence, in order to gracefully and with stealth, move in and out of circumstances and situations enabling him ultimately, and with impartiality, to marshal his skills to kill his prey. This is the story of such a predator with no conscience and with very bad intentions. He is paid handsomely because he is hired only for the highest-visibility assassinations that carry the most tantalizingly dangerous risks—in this case, the assassination of Charles de Gaulle, the President of France.

The Jackal takes it all in stride. He is part of the world only in its virtual state. He's here, and not here; it's the capstone of anonymity—of his invisibility.

The Main Story

The DVD describes the story this way:

> "... The Day of the Jackal tells of a cold, suave British assassin hired by the French OAS to kill General Charles de Gaulle. Nameless and faceless, the killer, known by the code name of Jackal relentlessly moves toward the date with death that would rock the world. The tension mounts as the methodical preparations of the Jackal are paralleled with the efforts of the police to uncover the plot. .."

It's 1963. The OAS (Organisation Armee Secrete, or, Organization of the Secret Army), the French underground's extreme right-wing nationalist militant organization, is violently protesting President Charles de Gaulle's support for Algeria's self-determination. The leadership of the OAS decided that the only way to stop this self-determination process underway for Algeria was to assassinate de Gaulle.

President de Gaulle's iconic stature that had emerged from the Second World War (he became the foremost emblem of resistance to the Nazis), meant that his support of the Algerian self-determination referendum was obviously going to carry the day. This would deprive France and the French population in Algeria from ever again controlling Algeria proper, the very thought anathema to the OAS.

Bastein-Thiry (played by Jean Sorel), is the OAS leader who, in concert with his compatriots, decides to retain a professional assassin to take out de Gaulle. Of several candidates, they decide on one who has a stellar resume as a contract killer and who has successfully plied his trade the world over. The OAS needs him because an earlier attempt on de Gaulle's life failed. To Bastein-Thiry's chagrin, although de Gaulle's car was riddled with bullets, he miraculously escaped unharmed. After the failed attempt, the remaining OAS leadership fled France and located themselves in a small Italian village.

Enter, The Jackal (played by Edward Fox).

The Jackal answers the OAS' invitation and visits this nest of extremists. He demands high payment for the job, which in turn creates the need for the OAS to plan a series of bank robberies in order to raise the money to pay him. The Jackal insists that no further contact with him will be permitted; they can only reach him with a phone number in Paris, and only by his Jackal name.

Expertise

Quickly, the Jackal gets to work. He is conscientious, and focused in a particularly single-minded way. He obviously knows what he's doing and one gets the feeling that this is experience exemplified. He is making every preparation necessary to successfully assassinate de Gaulle. And he's not afraid to do it. He wants to do it. He needs to do it. It's personal. Apparently, every such job is personal to him.

The Jackal goes about gathering his resources. He retains a gunsmith (played by Cyril Cusack) to construct an originally configured abridged rifle-like weapon with a telescopic sight. The weapon is designed to be assembled part by part so that each part can fit within the other, and then be inserted into elongated hollow cylinders. Once constructed, the Jackal will weld these cylinders onto the undercarriage of his automobile. Thus, should his vehicle be searched when he crosses any border, the weapon would not be discovered.

In addition, he acquires and assembles passports and forged papers, and assumes various facial disguises. He dyes his hair and selects the identities of people who have long ago died, or of individuals whose passports he has stolen. He soon has pictures of himself as an old man, a young man, and as he currently appears. All of it enables the Jackal to have as many options as possible, so that the probability of success in the pursuit of his goal is sky-high.

Throughout the process of preparing for the assassination, he is calm and collected and moves about with precision, in an accelerated manner, and with great élan. This is a man doing a job who doesn't at all understand the meaning of procrastination. He doesn't leave a stone unturned. He hits the books, doing library research and fieldwork, visiting a graveyard to identify the name, birth and death dates of the person he might impersonate. He is the perfect definition of goal-orientation and he spends time working on his anonymity. It's his job, his profession.

Isn't it that we are what we *do* and not who or what we *think* we are?

The Counterforce

The parallel action taking place includes a French authority structure galvanized to track him down. The most experienced of the Paris police force is called in. He is Claude Lebel (played by Michael Lonsdale). He doesn't look the part but he is really a first rate painstaking tracker who analyzes the smallest detail. The best at his job, Lebel is as logical and clever the Jackal—perhaps, even more so.

In a swift, clever maneuver, the French secret service captures one of the OAS couriers and tortures him. It is he who whispers the name "Jackal."

Talk about clever? The Jackal avoids hotels where he may be traced. He manages to endear himself to a beautiful married woman, Madame Colette de Montpellier (played by Delphine Seyrig), who he meets at a mountain lodge. He sleeps with her, finds out where she lives, and drives to her grand country estate. She is worried about his unexpected visit because Lebel had already driven to Madame Colette's estate and informed her of the police interest in the Jackal.

Apparently attracted to the Jackal, she confides in him and confesses that Lebel had informed her that he was a dangerous person. The Jackal, all cold and calculating, quietly strangles her. In an effort to avoid the police, he takes refuge at a Turkish bath house where no one would think to look for him. There, he picks up a homosexual man who invites the Jackal home. Now he has a roof over his head and is able to remain anonymous. However, when his face appears on television as a suspect in the murder of Madame de Mont-pellier, his host sees it. Of course, the Jackal must also kill him — and does.

Meanwhile, Inspector Lebel has begun to accumulate evidence of the Jackal's change of aliases. He further discovers that there is a leak of information aiding the Jackal and his OAS clients. Using phone taps, Lebel traces the leak to the Interior Minister's cabinet. This minister, while not guilty of collaboration with the enemy, is being controlled by a seductive woman who is a functionary of the OAS, and to whom he had revealed information of the ongoing Jackal saga.

Thus, the Jackal has now been informed by the OAS that he's been 'outed.' Fearing capture, the OAS decides to scrap the assassination plan altogether. The Jackal continues to elude the police and manages to slip out of several mishaps. Not knowing or especially caring that the plan has been aborted, the Jackal pursues his mission. That's who he is. He kills! With stealth! That's exactly what he needs to do.

He then drives to an intersection with one sign indicating a way out of France, and another indicating the way to Paris. Despite the presumed cancellation of the assassination, he decides to take the road to Paris. He's going to do what he does best! Again, he will pursue the goal of assassinating de Gaulle and he will do it on 'Liberation Day.' In fact, it's the idea of 'Liberation Day' that enables Lebel to sense the Jackal's plan.

Liberation Day

The entire area around the square where de Gaulle will honor the veterans of the resistance to the Nazis is monitored by scores of police, sharpshooters, and various other police personnel. All suspicious looking characters will be stopped. Crowds of people have now jammed the entire square.

The Jackal has infiltrated this chaos by disguising himself as an elderly man walking on crutches. His ankle is tied to the back of his thigh, covered by his trouser, so that he appears to be one-legged. With several medals pinned to his jacket, he appears to be a veteran of the war. He moves toward the building he spotted when he had done his reconnaissance. The top floor apartment of this building overlooks the square. It gives him a perfect trajectory toward where de Gaulle will be standing. He has already overheard that the occupant of that particular apartment is away. He is stopped by a gendarme (played by Philippe Leotard), who checks his papers, and then allows the Jackal to pass and enter the building.

He proceeds to kill the landlady, and immediately climbs the steps to the top floor. He opens the door and quickly begins to arrange the furniture so that he will be able to place his elbow on a hard stable surface, as he aims his rifle with the telescopic-sight, directly at de Gaulle's head.

The Jackal is ready.

Lebel comes across the same gendarme and realizes that it was probably the Jackal who the gendarme allowed to pass. They both rush to the Jackal's building and run up the stairs.

In the meantime, the Jackal fires his first shot. As he does, de Gaulle leans forward to kiss the first recipient of a medal and the Jackal's shot, right on target, continues on its trajectory and hits the ground. The Jackal is about to reload when the gendarme's machine gun blasts open the door and the two men rush into the room. The Jackal shoots the gendarme. Lebel goes for the gendarme's machine gun at the same time that the Jackal is reloading. They're about to shoot at each other but Lebel beats him to it. The Jackal is blasted completely off his feet across the room, hitting the far wall.

At the end of the film we see the Jackal in a casket being buried. Even in death no one knows who he was.

The Dying of the Light

The theme of anonymity resonates because it touches on the existential question of who we are in a vast universe that seemingly doesn't know us. We ask ourselves: 'What importance do I, as an individual, actually have considering that the universe is seemingly infinite?' Although we are not anonymous to those around us we are, in fact, aware that time will evolve into an endless horizon so that ultimately, each of us is entirely unknown unto eternity.

In other words, we ask, does any of it matter?

It is in that moment of haze when thinking about the vast universe and our minute place in it, we must jolt ourselves out of such reverie, tear ourselves away from contemplating ultimate nothingness, and return to our real lives—where we function, and think, and feel, and care, and do the best we can—and join the human race.

In the face of this existential horror, we protest the dying of the light. The very act of functioning, of carrying on relationships with other people, is itself our protest.

The Jackal doesn't care a whit about the dying of the light. He's the type of conspiratorial agent of those who *wants* the light to die, and he'll kill your light in such a way that you won't even have a moment to contemplate it. Poof, you're gone! He simply does his job, which is to increase the population of the dead, littered here and there around the earth—the assassinated ones.

As for the dying of his own light, because he is everyone (all sorts of different identities), he isn't really anyone in particular. He has no permanent relationships whatsoever. In this way, he is already figuratively not among us in this world, not alive in the sense that we know. For him, removed from any real social context, there is no question of "to be or not to be."

To Be Anonymous is to Be Invisible

There are some people who need to be popular; they must be known and seen. In benign cases, these types are gregarious, affable, and generally friendly. They value social interaction and love to participate in conversation. At the problematic extreme are those who crave nothing but attention, and want to be washed over with adulation.

The opposite inclination is seen in the Jackal's need for invisibility.

The Jackal on the Couch

When one seeks anonymity to the extent that they eliminate their identity in the world, they are acting out the invisibility need that was, for all intents and purposes, developed in childhood. At an early age such a child presumably felt ignored, or simply wasn't able to ask for things, or even feel entitled to be a full person. Inevitably, such a child would have little choice but to feel invisible, as though not important enough to be seen.

A child's personal experience of this feels at first like weakness. Gradually, such a sense of wandering aimlessly, here and there, and not being noticed by others, actually gets to

feel like strength. This is the crossover point where a person goes from existence in a social reality-world to an alternate existence in a kind of virtual state — as an anonymous person who doesn't need an identity — who feels seemingly invisible.

In adulthood, such invisibility feels empowering, especially if the person develops a skill in which invisibility becomes expertly implemented. A feeling of impunity then accompanies the nefarious range of activity from stalking to even killing. Anonymity and invisibility tend to validate this sense of power by nullifying any concern about rules and regulations. No longer guided by law and order, from their own invisible point of view, they therefore operate outside conventional ethics and morality.

In such a case, a failure to develop empathy early is at most, an issue of arrested development, or at least, becomes profoundly attenuated. In the Jackal's case, this important empathetic quality (and its usual function in social interaction) very likely became sacrificed — a classic example of stunted growth mostly inferred and perhaps even evidenced by the absence of conscience.

The Key

The key to the Jackal's inner life concerns what he had presumably internalized from childhood — silence. He absolutely needs to engage in endless externally stimulating situations in order to feel alive. It compensates for the inner silence. Without an animated inner life (silence), he must provide his own distraction through stimulation. His profession as a contract-killer allows him to be constantly in the throes of the excitement of his self-created unrelenting repertoire of external stimulations within the context of the absence of empathy and conscience in his personality.

Despite whatever charm and artifice such a person invokes, it's always in the service of some sort of psychopathic goal; in this case the constant stimulation on the outside in order to feel the absence of the terror of silence on the inside. And therefore, the Jackal is a classic case of a psychopath who only marches to the cadence of his own drummer. The Jackal's decision not to leave France, despite the instruction that the plan to assassinate de Gaulle was postponed or even cancelled, is an example of his decision to opt for excitement rather than be deprived of it. So he takes the turn and heads for Paris. His determination to finish the job has nothing to do with an ethical stand regarding responsibility. Rather, he'll do anything to avoid the inner silence; the higher the stakes, the more perilous the job, the better. To assassinate de Gaulle and then escape capture serves this purpose as nothing else could. And so this is definitely a solo act.

Finally, there remains the Jackal's need to project onto others what he feels about himself. Since he feels dead inside (silence), he's going to replicate this deadness with others. His need to sustain excitement on the outside in order not to feel deadened on the inside coincides with his need to have surrogates who are dead. In other words, to avoid the experience of his own inner silent life, he not only needs endless external stimulation, but also needs to externalize (project) his inside deadness onto the outside by killing others.

In the complete absence of empathy and conscience, it is this kind of self-serving depraved focus that becomes important. And so it is the others (those dead ones) who are silent. This need to be free of his own inner terror then becomes his primary motivation to express the power of his invisibility. And he validates this power in results—in his expertise as an assassin.

The moral of the story concerns the simple idea that one's early social development is highly correlated to one's future behavior, and that even children—especially children—need to be acknowledged, respected, treasured, and loved.

Otherwise, as the child is the father of the man, an ignored child can, as an adult, end up in Paris, with bad intentions.

Chapter 3

PREDATOR

(Released, 1987)

Screenplay by Jim Thomas / John Thomas
Produced by John Davis / Lawrence Gordon / Joel Silver
Executive Producer: Laurence Pereira
Associate Producers: Beau Marks / John Vallone
Original Music by Alan Silvestri
Directed by John McTiernan

Main Cast

Arnold Schwarzenegger	Dutch
Carl Weathers	Dillon
Elpidia Carrillo	Anna
Bill Duke	Mac
Jesse Ventura	Blain
Sonny Landham	Billy
Kevin Peter Hall	The Predator / Helicopter Pilot

Supporting Sample Cast

Richard Chaves	Poncho
R.G. Armstrong	General Phillips
Shane Black	Hawkins

Introduction

A group of American commandos led by Dutch (played by Arnold Schwarzenegger) is assigned to rescue captured airmen in a South American jungle. It's supposed to be a one-day operation—fly in by helicopter, get dropped to the ground by ropes dangling onto the jungle floor from the helicopter, grab the hostages, and escape by a pre-planned rendezvous with the helicopter.

The helicopter comes in low, drops the men, and they begin their trek into the jungle. The first thing they encounter is another helicopter that had crashed, part of which is impaled on high branches of a tree. They climb the tree and, judging from the grizzly evidence of human remains, infer that a fight had ensued in which several soldiers were killed. Soon thereafter, Billy (played by Sonny Landham), begins to sense something strange around them. Billy is gifted with a sixth sense and is apparently an experienced tracker but can't quite identify what it is that's bothering him. The group then finds other dead soldiers hanging by their feet from branches on a tree, completely stripped and flayed.

As this is happening, the audience can see that the Predator (played by Kevin Peter Hall), a translucent being, is watching them from a distant tree.

Dutch decides they must quickly find the hostages, rescue them, and then get the hell out of that place.

The Main Story

The DVD describes the story this way:

> ". . . [an] action-packed story of fighting men pitted against an unseen enemy, a force more power-

ful than their fiercest weapons. Recruited by the CIA to rescue hostages held by guerrilla fighters in a Central American country, [they] encounter an enemy unimaginably more deadly than any on Earth—because the Predator is not of this Earth."

The Fight Against the Guerrillas

Dutch and his men track the guerrillas to their compound. They encircle the compound and attack. The guerrillas fight back and the hostages are killed. Before the fight, while scouting out the compound, Dutch had witnessed the brutal execution of one of the hostages. The fire-fight continues in full-force and Dutch and his men methodically erase all resistance. They rescue Anna (played by Elpidio Carrillo) who knows more than she's saying. Dutch and his men find papers that reveal a plan they knew nothing about though Dillon, one of Dutch's men (played by Carl Weathers) did.

Apparently, Dutch and his men, who only volunteer for honorable missions, were sent to this God forsaken jungle under false pretenses. Had they been told the true nature of the rescue mission, they would have refused the assignment. Dillon and General Phillips (played by R.G. Armstrong) knew the real story—that the true purpose of the mission was to rescue a cabinet minister, and even more vital, to find important documents. Dutch is dismayed at being played, and confronts his erstwhile friend, Dillon, for not being a stand-up guy.

The Wounded Predator

They begin to move toward the rendezvous spot with the helicopter, still hoping to make a quick exit. Unfortunately, the

Predator is watching them—and wants them. Billy exclaims
what he can sense: "There's something in those trees." At that
point Anna tries to escape. She's pursued by one of Dutch's
men and in the process, the Predator kills him, skins him, and
it seems, even partially eats him.

For the first time, Anna sees the Predator in all its translu-
cence. The Predator kills another member of the team, and
again the Predator is seen. This time, the team responds with
rapid and massive fire power, and the Predator is wounded.
However, the Predator, seemingly a member of an advanced
alien species, can heal itself. As it heals, we see it in solid form
and notice that it wears some kind of body armor, and further,
applies a serum to its wounds.

The team deduces that the Predator is not human. Nothing could have survived the cumulative fire-power of all the remaining men on the team shooting continued rounds of ammo
in its direction. Anna says that the Predator bleeds and that it
can change color like a chameleon. Dutch answers that if it can
bleed, it can be killed.

Eventually the Predator is caught in an elaborate netting
trap but it easily escapes in one explosive attempt. The team
again tracks it and spots it on a high tree. Another of the men,
Mac (played by Bill Duke), after finding his good friend, Blain
(played by Jesse Ventura) killed by the Predator, is hell-bent
on killing the Predator. Of course, Mac is no match for the
Predator, and is quickly dispatched in the same way the others were. Soon, all the men have perished at the hands of
the Predator and have suffered the same fate—flayed and
possibly eaten. The only remaining member of the commando
team is Dutch, along with Anna. Even though Anna had been
hostile to Dutch and his contingent, as a result of the sadis-

tic action of the Predator, she has gradually become Dutch's ally. Dutch convinces Anna to get to the helicopter rendezvous spot while he remains behind in order to do combat with the Predator—mano-a-mano.

Dutch versus the Predator

Dutch tries to escape from the Predator's attack and falls into a river. He swims to shore and is about to crawl onto the muddy bank when he hears a loud splash. The Predator has been following Dutch and is now coming to get him. As Dutch climbs onto the muddy shore he's now covered head to toe with mud. The Predator also reaches the shore and carefully looks for Dutch but doesn't see him. Dutch realizes that it was because of his mud-covered body that the Predator couldn't see him.

In order to meet the Predator head on, Dutch knows he must seek an advantage, and begins constructing elaborate and deadly booby-traps into which he hopes to lure the beast. In the meantime we glimpse the beastly Predator ripping away at Billy's dead body and licking the skin of Billy's head until there is nothing left but a bare skull.

The climax of the film is the fight between Dutch and the Predator. The Predator is by far the stronger of the two (of course, with preternatural powers), and Dutch suffers a severe beating. In the end Dutch does in fact, lure the Predator into his booby-trap, and the Predator is dealt a decisive death blow.

However, the Predator comes equipped with the capacity to explode himself into an atomic-like bomb. He begins to set the bomb's timer for the explosion, but Dutch does a Jesse Owens and barely avoids being killed in the explosion. The incoming helicopter carrying Anna and General Phillips sees the explosion but still lands, rescues Dutch and they fly out of the jungle.

The Predator on the Couch

As the Predator is supposed to be an alien creature from an alien world, the story claims to be of a genre that posits this sort of possibility—that of invading alien creatures whose motives include conquering Earth people. We know of many such movies of aliens invading Earth—all with nefarious motives to destroy Earth people. In this story of the Predator, a simple descriptive analysis of the story would agree with such a characterization.

However, if we analyze the possible underlying meaning to the story—especially with a psychoanalytic view—another possible meaning emerges.

It's About the Nature of the Human

In this more psychoanalytic view, *Predator* can be seen as a story that plumbs the depth of the human character. It poses a question: If we tear away civilization and the rules and regulations of decent living, and dispose of police and other such agencies (such as parents)—agencies that put limits on behavior—what might we get?

One answer was given by William Golding in his influential novel, *Lord of the Flies.* After a plane crashes into a jungle there is an absence of civilization; rules and regulations of proper conduct are absent (no parents to guide the way), and man's nature (as played out in *Lord of the Flies* with a cast of children) turns nasty, power hungry, and gradually, quite sadistic. In the jungle, without civilization, we are in Conrad's *The Heart of Darkness*, where Kurtz says: "The horror, the horror."

Lord of the Flies is a story about children trying to survive the plane crash and then deciding how to organize themselves in order to survive in the jungle. Beneath the surface however, is a story about the ostensible true nature of man. In the film, *Predator*, the same theme can be seen to exist. On the descriptive story line, this Predator is a creature from outer space. In fact the opening scene of the movie is of a permeating night sky of stars. However, in another way, we can understand this creature from an outer-space place as really a projection, an externalization of the true nature of man as he exists in his own inner space; that is, the Predator is our own projection of what exists in us.

The Predator is us!

This predator shows up in the jungle—a place ostensibly without civilization. If we strip away civilized living, this can also be a metaphor for man's nature. In this philosophical sense, strip away civilization and what do you get? You get man who wants everything for himself. He'll even strip off your skin and eat your guts. He'll drink your blood.

In common everyday terms then, what is it in our basic uncivilized (or pre-civilized) selves that we want? In asking this question, *Predator* takes its place philosophically alongside literature like *Heart of Darkness* and *Lord of the Flies*.

The answer found in these stories is: I want everything; I want your money, your wife, your house, your success, your happiness. Want, want, want. According to this view of man, we're like that—avaricious, rapacious, we crave it all. Our needs rule, we are genetically programmed to primarily satisfy them for pleasure. The primary voice of the man's pleasure-need in man is—his wishes. What we basically wish for is to satisfy, gratify, and sate each and every cell of our bodies—as well as each and every of our wishful thoughts.

Thus, in this more profound sense, the Predator is not from outer space, he is from inner space, and he is telling us—that he is us. The underlying story here is really the naked one; without the controls of civilization, man's basic nature is to be covetous, to want everything others have, even their flesh. If necessary, we will, wolfishly and arbitrarily, take it all by force. We are a solo act!

At the End

At the end the face-off occurs: Dutch against the Predator. At the moment of their stand-off, the Predator removes its armored head-plate and reveals its face to Dutch. It's the face of an insect though enlarged, as if nuked and grotesquely swollen.

Dutch says: "You're one ugly mother-fucker." This could translate as: 'Underneath, this is what we all look like—ugly, self-serving, crude, and even unfamiliar—as though alien.'

Dutch also asks: "What the hell are you?" According to William Golding, Joseph Conrad, and the possible latent meaning of this movie, the possible answer is: "I am you!"

Dutch is winning the fight with the Predator when the Predator triggers the digital contraption strapped to its arm that shows some kind of code; it is a timing device that graphically reveals time is running out. In that moment, Dutch intuits that a bomb is about to detonate and trucks out of there full speed. He just makes it as the bomb goes off.

The simple moral of the 'beneath' story, might just be that raw nature doesn't die easily. If you can get to be civilized and not yield to ubiquitous feral instincts (presumably existing in all of us), then you're lucky. But the collateral point is that because of these instincts, no one really completely escapes their contaminating influences. Dutch, although banged-up, did get out of the jungle in one piece. The message is that civil living can triumph over base instincts and therefore there is hope for mankind—though the cost always lies in the remaining residual traces of those 'other' instincts.

Chapter 4

SUPERHEROES:
SUPERMAN/BATMAN/SPIDERMAN

Introduction

There is wrong-doing in the world and we all need help in having it corrected. There is unfairness in the world, and we know it needs to be rectified. Of course, the police are there to arrest the criminals who do the wrong-doing, but a lot of damage is usually done before these criminals are caught— assuming they are caught.

'Unfairness' is another story. Unfairness is frequently not an unlawful act as would be defined by legal statutes. 'Unfairness' is usually an abridgment of an implicit contract between people in which one of the parties has either insidiously or not, gained an advantage over the other. When this occurs, the implementation of some rectifier becomes experienced by the disadvantaged party as being absolutely necessary.

Such rectification of wrong-doing and acts of unfairness may elude police work or can be so subtle that the unfairness becomes just about impossible to cure. It generates a wish-fulness in people to want something magical, some outside force to intercede for them and gain some sense of redress; to remedy the situation by putting it right—the way it should have been right in the first place.

It may just be that children can tell us how to accomplish this empowering of disempowerment, and consequently put everything right again.

Enter, the superhero.

What Do Kids Know?

Kids know we need superheroes that can fly, are stronger than the criminals, and who even have ultra-special vision—even to the extent of anticipating danger. They want superheroes to restore normalcy after natural disasters strike—to fight back when the universe itself becomes unfair.

Children know full well that we definitely need to believe in such superheroes. They know because, as children, they are disempowered, small, and weak; in stark contrast, the world is powerful, and big, and strong. As kids, the world gave us our comic books and we devoured them.

Our superheroes were compensatory for what we were not. With respect to unfairness, these 'rectifiers' would always make things right. What a great relief it was to us that in identifying with them, they empowered or re-empowered us. They gave us strength in the form of temporary relief from the reality of our "disempoweredness." They gave us hope because they gratified our wishes. They did for us what we couldn't do for ourselves.

And there were any number of superheroes joining to support us in our eternal quest for empowerment: from Captain America, to Aquaman, to the Green Lantern, to Wonder Woman, to Daredevil, to the Green Arrow, to Blackhawk, to the Human Torch, to

Captain Marvel, to the Hulk, and of course, we cannot forget the Lone Ranger (and Tonto, too).

For our purposes, we will sample three of the most popular superheroes, so popular, that many decades after their creation they persist in various iterations in popular culture: Superman, Batman, and Spiderman, in chronological order of theatrical release:

SUPERMAN
(Released, 1978)

Story: Mario Puzo
Characters: Jerry Siegel/Joe Shuster
Screenplay:
Mario Puzo/David Newman/Leslie Newman/
Robert Benton/Tom Mankiewicz
Produced by Alexander Salkind/Pierre Spengler/
Richard Lester/Michael Thau
Associate Producer, Charles F. Greenlaw
Executive Producer: Ilya Salkind
Original Music, John Williams
Directed by Richard Donner

Sample Cast

Marlon Brando	Jor-El
Jackie Cooper	Perry White
Gene Hackman	Lex Luthor
Ned Beatty	Otis
Christopher Reeve	Superman/Clark Kent

Terence Stamp	General Zod
Margot Kidder	Lois Lane
Susannah York	Lara Lor-Van
Glenn Ford	Jonathan 'Pa' Kent
Jeff East	Young Clark Kent
Phyllis Thaxter	Martha Kent
Marc McClure	Jimmy Olsen
Valerie Perrine	Eve Teschmacher
Trevor Howard	First Elder

The Gist of It

Jor-El (played by Marlon Brando), knows that the red star, his home planet Krypton, is about to explode. He places his infant son, Kal-El, into a spacecraft headed to the planet Earth, in a distant solar system. Jor-El knows that Earth's atmosphere is similar to Krypton's, and its people look like the people of Krypton, so Earth will be a good new home for Kal-El. He also knows that the molecular structure of Kryptonites gives them superpowers when they are bombarded with rays from a yellow star.

Off goes the spacecraft, eventually landing on a farm in Kansas. It's the farm of Jonathan and Martha Kent (played by Glenn Ford, and Phyllis Thaxter). They find Kal-El, name him Clark, and raise him. Gradually, they see that Clark has superpowers and from time to time, Clark reveals this in spectacular fashion.

One day, as he nears adulthood, Clark is instinctively drawn to a green glowing crystal that he finds hidden in the barn. It is this crystal that compels Clark to travel to the North Pole where he discovers *The Fortress of Solitude*. The atmosphere there enables the crystal to ignite a process that transforms the entire configuration of Krypton so that Krypton itself becomes translucently materialized. Here, Clark's biological father, Jor-El, appears as a translucent vision. Jor-El relates Kal-El's history and offers his son the basic outlines of Kal-El's responsibilities on Earth—what he should and should not do.

After spending years assimilating all the necessary information, Kal El (as Clark Kent) returns to Metropolis, and lands a job as a reporter at the newspaper, *The Daily Planet*. Lois Lane is also a reporter there, and Clark is obviously attracted to her, but the attraction seems to be unrequited. As fate would have it, Clark saves Lois from a bizarre accident, in a way that requires him to display his superpowers. Of course, before Clark could save Lois, he needed to change into his Superman suit (cape and all). As Superman he has now revealed himself as a public figure: it is Lois who tags him with the "Superman" moniker.

Enter the evil one, Lex Luthor (played by Gene Hackman), whose malevolent plan is to destroy California with a nuclear missile. He does this in order to increase the value of his personal large land holdings that lie adjacent to California.

Luthor's girlfriend, Eva Teschmacher (played by Valerie Perrine) winds up saving Superman from Luthor's successful tactic of weakening Superman with Kryptonite. Eva frees Superman from his weakened condition but not before one of the missiles hits and creates a massive earthquake. Lois Lane is trapped in her car during the earthquake; her car is filled with rubble and she dies of suffocation. Superman, defying his father's warnings not to interfere in earthly matters, actually turns back time (we see Superman flying around the world so fast that the Earth starts spinning backward). It is possible that the Earth spinning backward is meant to indicate that Superman is traveling back in time by going faster than light-speed. By undoing what has already happened, Superman prevents Lois from getting her car trapped in the earthquake in the first place. Lois is alive!

Superman then captures Luthor and sends him to prison.

In the end, right wins and the 'rectifier' known as Superman offers us all a profound sense of re-empowerment. It effectively encourages us to possibly expect to have all of the disempowerment and helplessness in the world nullified.

BATMAN
(Released, 1989)

Story by Sam Hamm
Characters by Bob Kane
Screenplay by Sam Hamm/Warren Skaaren
Produced by Peter Guber/Jon Peters
Executive Producer: Benjamin Melniker/Michael E. Uslan
Co-producer: Chris Kenny
Associate Producer: Barbara Kalish
Original Music by Danny Elfman
Directed by Tim Burton

Sample Cast

Michael Keaton	Batman/Bruce Wayne
Michael Gouth	Alfred Pennyworth
Jack Nicholson	Joker/Jack Napier
Jack Palance	Carl Grissom

Kim Basinger	Vicki Vale
Jerry Hall	Alicia
Robert Wuhl	Alexander Knox
Tracey Walter	Bob the Goon
Pat Hingle	Commissioner James Gordon
Lee Wallace	The Mayor
Billy Dee Williams	Harvey Dent
William Hootkins	Lt. Echhardt

The Gist of It

It's Gotham City. The parents of a young boy are killed in its streets while the boy, Bruce Wayne, watches it all. This is the pivotal event that seals his fate as a crime-fighter. Fast forward to this boy as a man, who in his crime-fighting persona is Batman, cape and all.

At the same time that this Batman (played by Michael Keaton) begins his crime-fighting crusade, The Joker (played by Jack Nicholson) is up to no good.

Batman is different from Superman because Batman relies solely on natural ability—natural physical strength and skill, intelligence and inventive gadgets—that permit him to leap to high places and do all sorts of phenomenal acrobatics. Batman has no superpowers, and therefore invites greater concern on the part of the audience because of his human vulnerabilities.

He is the *Dark Knight*, a creature of the night. He operates in secret, out of a Bat Cave, on rooftops. We trust him and we depend on him. Although we know who he really is, we also identify with others who don't, but are eager to know. Vicky Vale, a photo journalist played by Kim Basinger, is the one most determined to unravel this mystery of the Batman.

The Joker is a lost soul; his accident in a chemical factory terribly disfigured him in such a way that he is now a raving lunatic hell-bent on wreaking havoc on Gotham City.

Of course, ultimately, the Joker is no match for Batman.

SPIDER-MAN
(Released, 2002)

Written by Stan Lee/Steve Ditko
Characters by Stan Lee/ Steve Ditko
Screenplay by David Keopp
Produced by Ian Bryce/Laura Ziskin
Executive Producer: Avi Arad/Stan Lee
Co-producer: Grant Curtis
Associate Producer: Heidi Fugeman/Steven P. Saeta
Original Music by Danny Elfman
Directed by Sam Raimi

Sample Cast

Tobey Maguire	Spider-Man/Peter Parker
Gerry Becker	Maximilian Fargas
Willem Dafoe	Green Goblin/Norman Osborn
Joe Manganiello	Flash Thompson
Kirsten Dunst	Mary Jane Watson
J.K. Simmons	J. Johah Jameson
James Franco	Harry Osborn
Cliff Robertson	Ben Parker
Bill Nunn	Joseph 'Robbie" Robertson

Jack Betts	Henry Balkan
Rosemary Harris	May Parker
Ted Raimi	Hoffman
Randy Savage	Bone Saw McGraw
John Paxton	Houseman

The Gist of It

He was an orphan since childhood and as a young man, was exposed to the murder of his uncle (played by Cliff Robertson). His innocence was exploited by bullies and he was too shy to approach his only love, Mary Jane Watson (played by Kirsten Dunst). He is Peter Parker (played by Tobey Maguire).

One day, in a freak accident, he is bitten by a radioactive spider. The next morning he awakens to find that he is now muscular and superhumanly strong, with the ability to adhere to walls and ceilings the way a spider does. He can even anticipate events of danger. He decides to fight crime and therefore eliminate the kind of evil that took his uncle before his time.

And so, Peter Parker becomes Spiderman.

Another character, Norman Osborn (played by Willem Dafoe), takes a potion and metamorphoses into the Green Goblin, a revenge-seeking altered psychotic 'bizarro' bent on killing Spiderman.

The story is essentially a duel, ending with the victorious Spiderman, supporter of justice, vanquishing the evil-doing Green Goblin.

Superheroes on the Couch

The Meaning of Dependency During Childhood

Throughout our childhood years we are in a very dependant position and a hard-core psychoanalytic principle is that dependency breeds anger. In order for a child to imagine some independence, frequently he will fantasize running away from home, or will identify with a story in which parents die. He must run away in order to escape stasis—and though dying is also an abandonment of those you love, it is also something usually not controlled by the one who dies. Therefore the dying person really can't be logically blamed for abandonment the way a parent can who forsakes a child and permanently leaves.

This issue is quite important in many classic superhero stories. Superman's parents were blown up with their planet, Krypton, Batman's parents were gunned down in the street, Robin's parents were killed, and Spiderman was an orphan since childhood. Each of these superheroes became free of parents. And isn't it true that in order for each of us to have become independent, we needed to leave home? Since children can't leave home, stories about orphaned children later becoming superheroes are appealing. This is especially true when time elapses in the story and through a series of accidents or incidents, the new adult acquires special powers.

Because of such 'loner' roots, superheroes are almost by definition solo performers, despite any love interests that develop.

The same symbolic event of independence occurs with Harry Potter, whose parents were killed, leaving Harry to more or less, fend for himself. Through a series of special events, Harry assumes magical powers. This, as we've seen, is the classic superhero creation myth.

From a psychoanalytic viewpoint, the fear of abandonment that all children experience is at some psychological depth really a concealed wish for independence. It is in fact normal, even when that wish for independence takes the form of parents dying, because dependency always breeds anger, and anger is an attack emotion that knows only one command—destroy! The awful fear in children of abandonment, of parents dying or disappearing, in addition to its literal meaning, can be a deep wish for empowerment. This is the reason for the success of superhero comic books. The child is easily able to identify with the protagonist, who is independent and therefore empowered to the extreme—strong and invincible, and who, to boot, defeats the bad guys.

But, Who Are the Bad Guys?

Now, the question is: Who are the bad guys in all of these superhero stories? It's an interesting question because the child will be fascinated with the ins and outs of what the bad guys are all about. What is it about the bad guy and his bag of tricks that attracts the child's attention? One psychoanalytic understanding is that the villain represents the child's bad impulses. Children are bombarded with a lot of stimuli they do not always understand which can usually undermine their ability to implement control of their impulses; since they cannot always define what they are experiencing, they don't know what controls to implement. In this way, the world can be confusing to them, even though they do have an instinctive sense of generally what is right and what is wrong.

Mature development in children can be defined as mastery over impulses; it is the postponement of gratification in the service of promoting long-range goals. The promotion of long-term goals begins to enable the child to gain social skills and to generally become an adaptive, normal social being, and simultaneously to inhibit 'bad' impulses.

The Rectification Club

In the quest to become an adaptive normal social being, bad impulses need to be civilized. And so, we get the *Rectification Club*. As far as the child is concerned, this *Rectification Club* is composed of superheroes who will tame all their bad impulses in the form of arresting, or defeating the bad guys. Membership in this club enables one to make wishes come true—wishes for good things to happen. It's all quite magical.

As adults, these movies still attract us and for the same reasons. Even as adults (and what children don't quite appreciate), we retain the sense that the world is quite full of variables that we can't control so that the superhero still resonates. Like the children we once were, we still retain the wish for mastery over these untoward variables.

The attraction of these superhero movies and the moral of such stories concerns the need to master our environment, to believe in the possibility of having wishes realized, to control our impulses, to believe that fairness should be sought, and to struggle with the idea of rectitude and empowerment. As adults we should know that only infrequently do our wishes get met, and even if we get our wish, it's not always met exactly or how we wished it—frequently not met to the fullest measure. We know that even though we're always living with thwarted or unfulfilled wishes of one kind or another, it's also true that the struggle to manage life, especially in the face of thwarted wishes, can be interesting and important, and that, for sure, struggle has value.

As adults, we try to develop a better ability to manage our fears and vulnerabilities so that we don't need to call on a superhero of the *Rectification Club*.

And by the way, who was that masked man?

Chapter 5

THE PASSION OF THE CHRIST
(Released, 2004)

Screenplay by Benedict Fitzgerald / Mel Gibson
Produced by Bruce Davey / Mel Gibson / Stephen McEveety
Executive Producer: Enzo Sisti
Original Music: John Debney
Directed by Mel Gibson

Main Cast

James Caviezel	Jesus
Maia Morgenstern	Mary
Christo Jivkov	John
Francesco De Vito	Peter
Monica Bellucci	Magdalen
Mattia Sbragia	Caiphas
Toni Bertorelli	Annas
Luca Lionello	Judas
Hristo Shopov	Pontius Pilate
Claudia Gerini	Claudia Procles
Luca De Dominicis	Herod
Rosalinda Celentano	Satan

The Passion of the Christ

Sample Supporting Cast

Fabio Sartor	Abenader
Paco Reconti	Whipping Guard
Adel Bakri	Temple Guard
Herod	Luca De Dominicis
Chokri Ben Zagden	James
Roberto Bestazzoni	Malchus
Adel Ben Ayed	Thomas
Pietro Sarubbi	Barabbas
Franco Costanzo	Accuser
Lino Salemme	Accuser
Maurizio Di Carmine	Elder
Francesco Gabriele	Elder
Omar Capalbo	Boy
Valerio Esposito	Boy
Roberto Visconti	Scornful Roman
Andrea Refuto	Young Jesus
Giovanni Capalbo	Cassius
Danilo Di Ruzza	Pilate's Servant
Vincenzo Monti	Herod's Courtier

Introduction

"By his wounds we are healed."

These are the words that introduce the story of the crucifixion of Jesus (played by James Caviezel). The film is an account of the last twelve hours of Jesus' life in which Jesus prays in the Garden of Gethsemane (the Garden of Olives) after the Last Supper.

In Mel Gibson's version of the story, *The Passion of the Christ,* virtually the entire film chronicles Jesus' bloody torture at the hands of the Romans due to the insistence of the Pharisees, especially Caiphas, the Jewish high priest (played by Mattia Spragia). Caiphas maneuvers Pontius Pilate (played by Hristo Shapov) to yield to demands for Jesus' crucifixion because Jesus is accused of blasphemy—he has announced he is the son of God. And thereafter, just about all of the movie is spent keeping the audience squirming, effectively captives, as they watch the vivid unrelenting torture of Jesus. Jesus is continuously and savagely whipped so that the crack of the lashes criss-cross his entire body, front and back, up and down, until he becomes a bloody living carcass.

The Roman soldiers, with their own brand of passion, sustain this ongoing beating of Jesus through flogging, gouging, caning, lashing, scourging, striking, binding. Finally, having him pilloried by nailing, hammering, and pounding spikes into his hands and feet, they attach him to the cross.

The Main Story

The DVD describes the story as:

> ". . . a profound story of courage and sacrifice depicting the final twelve hours in the life of Jesus Christ."

As characterized in this film, Pilate is a reluctant participant in the crucifixion story. Yet, he is complicit as Caiphas explicitly mentions Pilate's loyalty to Caeser could be called into question if Jesus were to be released. Even though Pilate's wife,

Claudia (played by Claudia Gerini), is sympathetic to the plight of Jesus, she is ultimately helpless to do anything that might convince Pilate to release Jesus. Such a release would deem Jesus innocent and undeserving of censure. However, Caiphas and his coterie, the Pharisees (the Jewish high priests), are characterized as having sway over Pilate and as actually extorting Pilate's power.

As a result of this discrepancy between the blood-thirsty Pharisees on the one hand and Pilate's almost merciful nature on the other, Pilate is depicted sympathetically as a person of principle. He wants to do the right thing but is forced into an unholy alliance with the Jewish priests to the point of capitulating to them. Yet he is curious, even unsure, and asks Jesus who he is, and then further, if he is truly King of the Jews, the Messiah? Jesus waits and then answers:

"I am the truth."

When Herod enters (played by Luca De Dominicis), Pilate blames Caiphas for the dilemma of what to do with Jesus. Herod refuses to condemn. In order to calm the rowdy crowd, and still perhaps in the hope of freeing Jesus, Pilate gives the crowd a choice: to free Jesus, or to free the thief, Barabbas (played by Pietro Sarubbi). This sudden strategy on the part of Pilate, who only wants Jesus chastised (and ultimately freed), provides additional evidence that in contrast, Caiphas wants Jesus crucified. Pilate is depicted as the lenient, more humane one.

The Roman soldiers are portrayed as barbaric, stupid, exaggeratedly uncouth and cruel. In addition, they are seen sweating profusely in their arduous and relentless task of brutalizing Jesus. In apparent contrast, the high Jewish priests don't expend a bit of energy. Therefore they are portrayed as the true cold-blooded culprits in this holy/unholy unfolding drama. The Pharisees feel Jesus is a threat to their way of life and to their power. They are particularly concerned and even contemptible of him because of his claim that he is King of the Jews, the true Messiah.

The Words of Jesus

Throughout the agony of his torture, Gibson gives us flashbacks of Jesus proclaiming the "word." He refers to "betrayal" and during the Las Supper, he intones:

"Love thine enemies."

On the cross, in addition to praying for the "Father" to defend him, we hear his last seven emanations:

1. "Father forgive them, for they know not what they do";
2. "Today you will be with me in paradise";
3. "Behold your son; behold your mother";
4. "My God, my God, why have you forsaken me?";
5. "I thirst;"
6. "It is finished";
7. "Into your hands I commit my spirit."

And then there is Satan, the Devil, (played by Rosalinda Celentano) appearing in the form of a woman. This Satan predicts that Jesus will not be able to withstand the punishment, but, even this Devil is especially interested in Jesus' lineage. She asks:

"Who is your father?"

Apparently, Satan intuits, and even knows, what she doesn't want to know — what she is afraid to know.

With Satan watching, Jesus is beaten by the Roman soldiers. Jesus says:

> "My heart is ready, Father."

And So It Was The Way It Was Supposed To Be

According to prophecy, it was Judas Iscariot (played by Luca Lionello), who betrays Jesus and does so for a mere thirty shekels. (Of course, it is Caiphas who pays him.) When Jesus acknowledges Judas' betrayal, the Roman soldiers promptly apprehend him and take him away to face his fate. Judas, in a state of severe remorse, wants to return the treasure. He is looking for some measure of redemption. However, the Pharisees refuse to partake of any act that even in the remotest way would compromise their indictment of Jesus, especially not his incarceration.

When Jesus' followers see him apprehended, they attack the Roman soldiers but Jesus orders them to stop. He proclaims:

> "Those who live by the sword shall die by the sword."

Mary, his mother (played by Maia Morgenstern), sees his agony and says:

> "It has begun, Lord, so be it."

Jesus speaks as the Son of God and is spat upon and beaten by the Jewish priests. Terror strikes his disciples and

Peter (played by Fransesco De Vito) experiences exactly what Jesus had told him—that Peter will deny Jesus three different times. In the meantime, Judas' drama unfolds in a horrible way. He is plagued by Satan's disciples and cruelly haunted by ugly hallucinations and delusions until he finally hangs himself.

Apparently, according to this particular version of the crucifixion of Jesus, Gibson has the Roman soldiers engaged in nothing less than extraordinary gratuitous violence which mother Mary witnesses. In addition, the "Crown of Thorns" is pushed and pressured onto Jesus' head, his face and head are punctured, dripping ringlets of blood onto his face.

As is expected, Jesus is forced to carry the cross. He is barely able to stand but he is whipped and pushed and forced to his feet and still he carries the cross to Golgotha. The Devil follows along as does Mother Mary and Mary Magdalen (played by Monica Belluci). Mary Magdalen has a flashback of when Jesus first found her and saved her. People along the way are crying and pleading for it all to cease. Mother Mary then speaks to Jesus, and he says to her:

"See, mother, I make all things new."

Jesus is crucified in the most horrible and cruelest manner. An earthquake ensues, and apparently this is Gibson's exclamation point—a warning to everyone that a convulsion of the first order has occurred and that although prophesized, it nevertheless indicates something impossibly wrong has occurred.

In the closing scene, the tomb in which Jesus was interred is now, after three days, vacant. Jesus has vanished—and has been, as prophesized—resurrected.

As Jesus says:

"It is accomplished."

Mel Gibson on the Couch

There is a psychology to righteous indignation, and Mel Gibson understands it. He knows exactly how to ignite the audience's rage and demand for blood — for maximum revenge. He has displayed this sort of virtuosity in many of his films. These include: *Braveheart*, *Payback*, *The Patriot*, *Ransom*, *Edge of Darkness,* and of course, here, in *The Passion of the Christ.*

The question is: What is Gibson's secret to getting the viewer to only feel satisfied if the good guys can get even with the bad guys — and then do to the bad guys, in spades, what was done to them? According to the predictable story line, what was done to the good guys was unusually heartless and entirely uncalled for. And yes, of course, the horror and the cruelty is in fact experienced by the audience, because the viewer is naturally identifying with the innocent — the one that was unjustly hurt, scarred for life, and always for no culpable reason.

What Gibson has actually identified is the secret of what 'makes' anger — the secret of what must happen in order for the audience to feel absolute justification in the expectation of the extreme violence that is surely awaiting the bad guy. By the time the expected takes place the audience needs it — is almost aching for it!

Therefore, by this time, what is the audience waiting for? The answer is that the audience, after witnessing such monumental injustice, is now needing a grizzly retribution—and is feeling a fury to the point of a genocidal rage.

It's About Helplessness

The secret, of course, concerns Gibson's manipulation of the audience's ubiquitous response to the condition of extreme helplessness. Another hard-core principle is that helplessness breeds rage, and therefore, the condition of extreme helplessness breeds extreme rage. No one wants to feel helpless, because in the condition of helplessness, one is disempowered.

Here is where Mel Gibson reigns supreme. He is particularly masterful in knowing how to render the innocent person as a helpless soul who becomes wantonly and cruelly treated—agonizingly punished as, when a loved one (child or spouse), without any recourse whatsoever, is summarily killed. Or, if not killed, then terribly tortured, and then perhaps kept indefinitely in that state of utter helplessness and disempowerment, in visible unmentionable agony.

The point is that as long as the innocent one is kept suffering in a helpless and faultless condition, Gibson can keep such molten anger sustained both in the protagonist as well as in the audience. As a matter of fact, the victim in the story is sometimes so numbed with pain that for such a person to think of revenge is an irrelevancy because the boiling vat of pain is so severe that the victim cannot think past his suffering.

The thinking is left to the audience viewing this catastrophic episode of pain. The viewer knows that it's only on the screen in a movie, and yet, can think about the 'sweeeeeeet' and now necessary and absolute justice of vengeance. The punishment must, must, must equal the crime, and then some.

Viewers need that revenge because even though it's not happening to them personally, they've been infected with indignant righteousness that can only be assuaged through reprisal—a reprisal of redress—of maximum retaliation. In the face of such righteous vengeance, getting even is not enough; that is to say, the cruel must not only be soundly defeated, they must, also, be aware of the humiliation of this defeat. At the moment of experiencing such humiliation, the cruel must also be killed—slowly, excruciatingly and dramatically—with emphasis, and with significance. At the bitter end, even if Gibson should decide to grant clemency, the audience is nevertheless left in an ambivalent state—relieved for a moment, but still imbued, proselytized, and thoroughly infected with the memory trace of the desire to kill.

Either way, this is Gibson at his best.

Are the Sons Responsible For the Sins of the Father?

Of course, *The Passion of the Christ* is a story about a son and a father. If the sons are implicated in the sins of the father, this, of course, is not relevant to Jesus and his Father because the father in Jesus' case is sinless. However, in Mel Gibson's life, his father, Hutton Peter Gibson, was a major factor in Gibson's theological grounding. It is generally known that Gibson senior is a devout Christian—a literal Catholic who believes every word of the Bible as though written by God. Contradictions mean nothing, even if one Gospel does not coincide with another, or if facets of stories are contradictory or asymmetrical from one Gospel to the other.

In addition, Mr. Gibson senior has been known to be obsessed with conspiracy theories involving the Vatican, Jews, unseen forces that he believes remotely controlled the events of the World Trade Center catastrophe of 9/11. He has also questioned the veracity of certain Holocaust claims, namely the claim of the six million Jews killed. In addition, he has been accused of anti-Semitism, and despite making anti-Jewish remarks, he nevertheless has denied the accusation.

The gist of it all seems to be that Gibson senior is an exasperated person who feels that at almost every turn his wishes have been thwarted by forces that are not within his control. This also applies to his views on how the United States government acts with respect to its obligations, or how the Masonic organization implicates Jewish membership in nefarious plots, or how the second Vatican Council ostensibly falsified its selection of a Pope, preferring the liberal one to the conservative, who, Gibson senior claims, actually won.

Psychologically, when one incessantly needs their personal wishes and desired outcomes to be gratifyingly in concert—that is to say, perfectly correlated—and rather the opposite occurs, then that person will be very angry and will in most cases feel preoccupied with a getting-even sensibility. This kind of abject disappointment is the soil in which hatred germinates and further, such utter disappointment is the lever that releases a consistent generated feeling of righteous indignation about almost everything.

In any event, Mel Gibson refuses to discuss his father. His loyalty is understandable as a son's supportive attitude in not permitting his father to appear anything other than admired and strong. It could be that Mel Gibson is stubborn about not yielding to pressures to 'out' his father as some sort of quack. Instead, as could be the case in many such father/son relationships, the son frequently assumes a compensatory stance in support of the father, and, in fact can have a fuck-you attitude toward a world that seems to ridicule and hold such a father in low esteem. There is evidence to suggest that Mel Gibson shares his father's displaced exasperation, for example when he spouted anti-Jewish sentiments to a traffic officer who stopped him because of his inebriated state.

Given such loyalties between sons and their fathers, the question can be asked as to whether the son can be held responsible for the sins of the father—assuming the father has been capable of, and culpable in sin. And since the father/son Gibson relationship is not of the same nature as the relationship of Jesus to his Father, then we might assume that by any standard of Catholic Christian belief, Hutton Gibson's attitudes and behavior can possibly contain elements that could be considered 'sin' whereas the same could not be said of Jesus' Father.

Therefore, we need to pose the question to Mel Gibson directly.

> "Are you, Mr. Gibson, responsible for the sins of your father, Hutton? And by sins I guess we're referring to attitudes and relatively benign behaviors, not that your father has committed any punishable felony."

Psychoanalytically, the principle answer for any son probably should be in the affirmative. Yes, the sons are indeed, and resoundingly so, responsible for the sins of the father—insofar as the sons are responsible to not repeat the sins of the father.

What this really means is that in the service of progress children will hopefully do better than their parents. In the Gibson dyad of father/son, it seems that in many of his films, Mel Gibson has an apparent need for terrible vengeance resulting from intense righteous indignation in the dramatic staging of the cruelest cruelty to an innocent person. He seems to need to exact the finest calibration of revenge—to squeeze out that last drop of blood. It is very possibly an acting-out of the father's wishes through the child. Gibson junior is possibly expressing for Gibson senior what Gibson senior couldn't satisfy for himself. And it's being done by a lone person—by Mel Gibson giving his father gift after gift of getting even with the conspirators.

This movie, *The Passion of the Christ*, is therefore considered in the category of *Solos* despite the references on the one hand, between Jesus and his Father, and on the other, between Mel Gibson and his father. The entire rendition of this version of *The Passion of the Christ,* is devoted entirely to the audience's personal visual evidence of Christ's agony minus any retribution by another character in the story, or by the father, God himself. Therefore, since retribution for such evil is irresistible, Gibson leaves the audience with the task of achieving such retribution—thinking about, and seeking, those responsible. Guess who?

Yes, it's a psychological connection of father and son, but the deed is accomplished only by one of them and therefore, Gibson's treatment of *The Passion of the Christ* is a perfect template for the entire vengeful need seen in so many of his films. The first to come to mind is *The Patriot,* in which the wrath of the father becomes perfectly clear in a savage scene where Gibson (as the father) butchers the British soldiers with an axe, chopping them to pieces in a fit of furious retributional rage. It is a righteous expostulation, a singularly vicious feast of vengeance for the abject and even arbitrary murder of his young son by specific order of the British Colonel Tavington. The point of such retribution is that the father's wrath is inflamed to the maximum because of his innocent son's cruel death.

The moral of this Mel Gibson portrait on the psychoanalytic couch, tells us that with respect to one's personal life, heroics don't always mean autonomy or independence from the original family drama. True heroism concerns whether sons and daughters are helped by the previous generation to actually strive to do better. By the same token, we ask whether the new generation can help the previous generation do better as well—even for the son to help the father be a bit different, a bit better.

One generation helping the other could, in turn, help delete the "indignation" from the "righteousness", and move us all away from genocidal hatreds that incite and gratify needs for severe retribution. Could it then be possible that the move away from such needs for vengeance and hatred can instead, be a step in the direction of Christian forgiveness—or perhaps be a step in correcting historical misinformation?

Which is healthier, which is a better teaching, Mr. Gibson—the hatred inherent in righteous indignation, or Christian forgiveness and the correcting of historical misinformation?

PART 2

DUETS

Chapter 6

WHEN HARRY MET SALLY
(Released, 1989)

Original story and screenplay by Nora Ephron
Produced by Rob Reiner/Andrew Scheinman
Co-produced by Steve Nicolaides/Jeffrey Stott
Associate Producer: Nora Ephron
Music arranged by Marc Shaiman
Special musical performances and arrangements:
Harry Connick Jr.
Directed by Rob Reiner

Sample Songs
It Had To Be You.
Performed by Frank Sinatra
Our Love Is Here To Stay.
Performed by Louis Armstrong and Ella Fitzgerald
Let's Call The Whole Thing Off.
Performed by Louis Armstrong and Ella Fitzgerald
Where Or When.
Performed by Ella Fitzgerald

But Not For Me.
   Performed by Harry Connick, Jr.
Don't Get Around Much Any More.
   Performed by Harry Connick, Jr.

Main Cast

Billy Crystal	Harry Burns
Meg Ryan	Sally Albright
Carrie Fisher	Marie
Bruno Kirby	Jess

Sample Supporting Cast

Steven Ford	Joe
Lisa Jane Persky	Alice
Michelle Nicastro	Amanda
Gretchen Palmer	Stewardess
Robert Alan Beuth	Man on Aisle
Joe Viviani	Judge
Harley Jane Kozak	Helen
Kevin Rooney	Ira
Franc Luz	Julian
Tracy Reiner	Emily
Estelle Reiner	Older woman in diner ordering what Sally had

Documentary Couples

Kuno Sponholz	Connie Sawyer
Charles Dugan	Katherine Squire

Al Christy   Frances Chaney
Bernie Hern   Rose Wright
Aldo Rossi   Donna Hardy
Peter Pan   Jane Chung

Introduction

This is a love story told through words and popular music, as we shall see. First however, we need to ask:

Can men and women be friends?

Harry Burns (played by Billy Crystal) doesn't think so. Harry cynically boils it down to sex; that is, men and women can't be friends because sex is always hovering over the two as the unspoken motive, or even, impulse driving the relationship. Yet, this movie begins with short documentary footage of an elderly couple telling the unseen interviewer behind the camera that they've been married for 50 years and it was love at first sight. And with that we get Louis Armstrong singing *Our Love Is Here To Stay* ("It's very clear, our love is here to stay. . . ."). Of course this is a harbinger of things to come, especially as illustrated throughout the film by elderly couples who talk to the camera with the same message: love can be here to stay.

Even though love might be here to stay, the truth of it all is that on a ten-point scale, the best any marriage can be is an eight. But that's okay folks, because despite what Harry expects, there's no such thing as a ten—or even a nine. The reason for this rather less than perfect "A" is that in marriage we're dealing with two different personalities, each of which contains its own particular psychological immune system. The cold fact is that at some point in any two-person primary relationship (such as a marriage) these immune systems are going to clash. And clashing means anger and rejection.

Thus, we've got to remember that life begins to chip away at all primary relationships including marriage, and as a result, spouses feel as though they're suffering inordinately. The fact is, they probably are suffering because basically it takes perseverance to try and fit the bumps in your head to the holes in your partner's head, or vice versa. It all takes living with the discomforts until they're worked on and worked out—at least reasonably so. If you can get to an eight, that's pretty damn good.

As far as Harry is concerned, not just sex, but anything can ruin a relationship so the idea of something being perfect becomes essentially irrelevant. Get it, Harry? That's why there's a "for better or worse" clause in every marriage ceremony. You think that's because it always gets better?

The Main Story

The DVD describes the story as:

> "Will sex ruin a perfect relationship between a man and a woman? That's what Harry and Sally debate during their trip from Chicago to New York. And eleven years later, they're still no closer to finding the answer. Will these two best friends ever accept that they're meant for each other. . .or will they continue to deny the attraction that's existed since the first moment *When Harry Met Sally*?"

Can Men and Women be Friends?

It's been arranged that Sally Albright (played by Meg Ryan) and Harry will drive together to New York City. It's 1977. After graduation from the University of Chicago, they're sharing the drive to their respective new lives. Harry will be a political consultant and Sally will pursue her dream of being a journalist.

On the way, Harry does a Woody Allen and philosophizes (actually pontificates) about why a friendship between a man and a woman can't work. Sex! Harry and Sally talk openly about sex. And Harry essentially cleans up an old favorite joke of single men—to wit: What's the fastest thing in the world? The answer is: The amount of time it takes after sex for a man to hit the door after his orgasm. And this means that all the man wanted was sex and nothing else; not conversation, not snuggling, not smoking, not, kissing, not, not, not! This sums up how Harry feels. He is certain that because sex is the 800 pound gorilla in the room, men and women definitely cannot be friends—and notwithstanding possible exceptions, this might be a point not to be easily scoffed at.

Harry and Sally reach their New York City destination and then part. Somewhere along the line, Louis Armstrong begins to sing, *Let's Call the Whole Thing Off.*

It's five years later and they run into one another at an airport. At this point Ella Fitzgerald begins singing *Where or When?* They remember. They both have other relationships, in fact, Harry is about to be married. They begin to chat and again Harry proclaims that men and women simply cannot be friends because of the sex thing.

Five more years elapse, and this time they meet in a bookstore. Here, Sally is telling her friends Marie (played by Carrie

Fisher), and Alice (played by Lisa Jane Persky), that she and Joe (the guy she was with when she met Harry five years earlier at the airport) have broken up. Elsewhere, simultaneously, Harry is confiding to his buddy, Jess (Played by Bruno Kirby), that Helen (who he was about to marry when he and Sally met at the airport five years earlier) walked out on him—as it turned out, for another man.

Meanwhile, Marie spots Harry spying on Sally from across the bookstore. Marie says: "Someone is staring at you in 'Personal Growth.'" We hear Frank Sinatra singing, *It Had To Be You*, and it becomes clear—from that point on, Harry and Sally will be ascending the difficult terrain leading to permanent togetherness. Just to underscore the point, we again also hear *Our Love Is Here To Stay.* Harry, thinking he may have a cold, says he thinks he's coming down with something. Ha. What he's coming down with is the start of the defeat of his cynicism regarding relationships and a corresponding uphill struggle to get to Sally, whom he really loves.

Yay, They're Friends

Lo and behold, they begin to talk, and they become friends; actually good intimate special friends—the kind of friends that a marriage could definitely use. They're considerate to one another, concerned about one another, and very importantly, they listen to one another. At some point, in keeping with their good intentions for one another, Harry decides that Sally should meet Jess, and Sally decides that Harry should meet Marie. The four of them go out together, and the shidduch (match) turns into tepid water. Jess and Sally have zero interest in one another, while Marie and Harry have even less interest in one another. However, Jess and Marie are apparently made for each other and immediately hit it off. Soon, while Harry and Sally are agonizing over this or that and dating other people, Jess and Marie are planning a wedding.

And then it happens. Sally discovers that her old boyfriend, Joe (played by Steven Ford), is getting married and she falls apart. She calls Harry, Harry comes over to comfort her, and in the context of this understanding and togetherness, they have sex. In the background we again hear: *It Had To Be You*.

But Harry's problem persists. The actual consummation of the Harry/Sally circuitry puts Harry in a trance of regret. He lies there next to her, after making love staring off into space and begins answering all of Sally's questions with monosyllabic yeses or nos, while at the same time, Sally is walking around in love. In the morning as Sally awakens, she sees Harry getting ready to leave. Harry's felt suffocated and he kind of makes himself scarce. When they do get together for dinner, Harry says that it's so nice to eat with someone and not have to talk. So, they don't meet for a while and it seems they grow apart.

Of course, they again meet at Jess and Marie's wedding where Harry is Best Man, and Sally, Maid of Honor. As expected they have a spat and again separate. Then, after a while, Harry asks her out for New Year's Eve, but she turns him down.

On New Year's Eve, all alone, Harry begins walking the streets. He spots a couple kissing and we hear Harry Connick Jr. in the background singing, *But Not For Me (They're writing songs of love, but not for me. . . .)*. Harry begins to tear away his resistance to a more permanent relationship with Sally and suddenly begins racing to the New Year's Eve party in order to get there before the clock strikes twelve.

Harry makes it on time, they see one another, he confesses his love for her as well as his enchantment with all of her delightful idiosyncrasies, and he indicates that he wants to spend the rest of his life with her.

He does, and that's it folks—except for another great song, Sinatra singing—*It Had To Be You.*

Harry Burns on the Couch

"Will sex ruin a perfect relationship between and man and a woman?" That first sentence of the DVD contains a powerful word. The word is "perfect." Yes, this issue of "perfect" is the key to the entire dilemma of Harry and Sally not connecting in a permanent way. Instead they winnow away the time here and there with life's vicissitudes and in various endeavors—some important, some not. It's an example of how people, in this case, Harry, can squander more than a decade avoiding the very conflict that he will later confront and possibly conquer.

The question is why is the word "perfect" the key to the entire story and to Harry's insistence that because of sex, men and women can't be friends? The psychoanalytic answer is that fundamentally, the issue of perfection basically refers to an entire psychology focused on childhood. What this means is that as adults, we are always carrying around residual unfinished promises; every one of our incomplete and unfulfilled wishes of childhood still needs to be satisfied. In other words, we won't be happy until those unfinished and unrealized things get satisfied. And if they do get done, then that's the definition of "perfect." But, of course, the bad news (or is it the good news?) is that they will never all be completed or satisfied.

So, in a word, "perfect" always refers to childhood, whereas "good" always refers to present-day adulthood. And this idea of the "perfect" as relegated to the past, while the "good" is related to the present, clarifies the aphorism: 'The perfect is the enemy of the good.' This means that a person who insists on perfection in relationships in the present, is doomed not to have any. It is an attempt to proceed in life without first satisfying age-old unfinished business. When that age-old business is finished, that perfects what once was, and so one's implicit logic is that now that the old stuff has been satisfied, we can get going on the newer current stuff.

Of course, such logic is wishful thinking because most frequently the old stuff can't really be fixed that way. By insisting it can, one squanders time in their present adult life by criticizing everything that isn't perfect. It's a psychoanalytic truth that such a critical eye toward everything in the present is really a defensive attempt (and usually a successful one) not to easily enter any relationship. In other words, the person's insistence on the "perfect," is really a resistance against leaving the past; it's a resistance against leaving childhood.

And that's exactly where Harry Burns lives — in the past, in childhood. In reality, in order to fall in love and have a relationship, one must be able to incorporate the partner's various imperfections, and also accept one's own imperfections. And that's all good enough, even if it's not perfect.

Shrink Talk to Harry

So, will sex ruin a perfect relationship between a man and a woman? The psychoanalytic answer is yes, Harry, sex and everything else will ruin any relationship provided that at least

one of the partners (you) insists on the prerogative of sole loyalty to remaking everything in your childhood that you always
felt needed remaking. In that way you can feel that you've gotten everything you ever wanted and that then everything was
perfect. The problem is that in this perfectly satisfied relationship with your childhood, it's you with you, and no one else
is involved. You're having a perfect relationship with yourself,
Harry!

In adult life, childhood complaints brought into relationships
is an accident waiting to happen. In psychoanalytic language
it's called "transference"—you attribute all these unfinished
and thwarted wishes and needs from childhood onto your current experience. For example, in your relationship with Sally,
you consider sex to be the stumbling block to the friendship / relationship. Your reasoning, Harry, if you don't mind me saying
so, is nonsense. It's got nothing to do with sex. In a primary relationship such as marriage, if there's trouble in the bedroom,
and the bedroom door shuts, it's actually never the bedroom
(sex) that was the cause of the trouble.

Rather, when the bedroom door shuts, it's really what's
happening in the living room that is the real problem. So the
question is: What should be happening in the living room that
isn't happening? The answer is simple: not just listening, but
hearing; not just talking but conversing; and, not always solving
your partner's problems but rather trying to reflect their feelings
so that they will feel, and be, understood. It means expressing
affection, being available, pitching in, and not behaving like an
adolescent boy. Get it, Harry? In a relationship you've got to
put your shoulder to the wheel, and make that wheel turn.

Remember, Harry, men get kind of passive in the house.
Know why? It's because deep down they want to be mothered,

taken care of. You've got to resist that, Harry. You've got to move your ass in a relationship and not come off as lethargic or inert. And you don't have to wait to do something until she (in this case, Sally) asks you to do it. Don't wait! Do it yourself before you're asked because, of course, it's obvious that you know what needs to be done.

If you behave like an adolescent boy, how do you expect her to respect you? Make no mistake about it, in order for that bedroom door to remain open, she will need to respect you. So when you came over to Sally's because she was distraught, you, in turn, were kind, affectionate, and understanding, and also reflected her feelings, and listened to her and became part of the conversation. All of that contributed to great intimacy and then of course, you both, as friends, did the unmentionable sex thing. Here's where it went wrong. After the sex, you satisfied a self-fulfilling prophecy by going into a funk. The reason you went into that funk was because you simply weren't ready for this adult ever-waiting phase of your life. In other words you were stubborn, and it was that transference thing—you weren't ready to give up the relationship between you and you.

See what I mean?

So, now when we return to your original position regarding sex preventing a man and a woman from being friends, we can see that there's a lot more to it than you first thought. Let's follow the music; the songs show the dichotomy of your psychological life very well. If we sample just some of them we get songs that refer to the hope of relationships even in the absence of any consideration of perfection: *It Had To Be You*, and, *Our Love Is Here To Stay*. Then we also have songs about resistance to a relationship, feeling bereft of one: *Where or*

When, or, 'They're writing songs of love,' *But Not For Me*, and finally, the ultimatum song, *Let's Call The Whole Thing Off*. And then you're left with aloneness as in *Don't Get Around Much Any More*.

But in the end, Harry, the good news was that your concern about the "perfect" was not in any way related to narcissism. You were just immature. But you eventually worked through your perfection-childhood-stubbornness, and you married Sally, and then you and Sally also spoke to the camera as a duet, a happily married couple.

So, what's the moral of the story? I guess it would have to be that the perfect is indeed, the avowed enemy of the good. And by the way, Harry, I think that you and Sally make not just a good couple, but a great one.

Congratulations.

Chapter 7

HUSBANDS AND WIVES
(Released, 1992)

Produced by Robert Greenhut
Executive Producer: Charles H. Joffe/Jack Rollins
Associate Producer: Thomas A. Reilly
Co-producer: Helen Robin/Joseph Hartwick
Music selected by Woody Allen
Written and Directed by Woody Allen

Main Cast

Woody Allen	Prof. Gabriel 'Gabe" Roth
Mia Farrow	Judy Roth
Judy Davis	Sally
Sydney Pollack	Jack
Juliette Lewis	Rain
Liam Neeson	Michael Gates
Blythe Danner	Rain's Mother
Lysette Anthony	Sam—Jack's Girlfriend

Sample Supporting Cast

Cristi Conaway	Shawn Grainger—Call Girl
Timothy Jerome	Paul—Sally's Date

Ron Rifkin	Richard—Rain's Analyst
Bruce Jay Friedman	Peter Styles
Jeffrey Kurland	Interviewer—Narrator
Benno Schmidt	Judy's Ex-husband
Brian McConnachie	Rain's Father
Nick Metropolis	TV Scientist
Ron August	Rain's Ex-lover
John Bucher	Rain's Ex-lover
Matthew Flint	Carl—Rain's Boyfriend
Philip Levy	Taxi Dispatcher
Jerry Zaks	Dinner Party Guest
Nora Ephron	Dinner Party Guest
Connie Picard	Banducci Family
Steven Randazzo	Banducci Family
Tony Turco	Banducci Family
Adelaide Mestre	Banducci Family

Introduction

To learn about the real stuff of relationships it would be difficult to find a better, more brilliant exegesis than *Husbands and Wives*. The outside world never knows what goes on behind closed doors. You think certain friends are so happy and then you hear they've split up. Or good friends surprise you with the disclosure that: "He slept on the living room couch last night."

The fact is that men and women are nurtured differently by the world, leading to what is known as acculturated gender differences. The result is that if men feel humiliated instead of adored they will also feel terribly inadequate. Women feel the same kind of inadequacy if they are made to feel wrong.

Any relationship that is able to absorb the give and take and the shocks of relationship events, and for men not to be unduly furious at even the slightest hint of a slight put-down, and for women not to endlessly continue the discussion because they need to be right, requires this audience of one to the other (the couple) to be sturdy, and hearty.

If the relationship is to be sustained, then at least one of the partners needs to be able to suffer—inordinately. If one of the partners can do this the couple will have a chance. If both can do it, then they are a sure thing. If neither can. . . .well, the outcome is 50 percent divorce rate in the U.S.A. with another 30 percent hanging by a thread.

The Main Story

The DVD describes the story this way:

> "...two New York couples re-examine their marriages and find themselves wanting more . . . the long-married [couples'] . . . own relationship starts to crumble when their best friends ... announce they're separating. They immediately pair up with younger, sexier paramours and enjoy again the pleasures of fresh passion. But smoldering resentments and unexpected jealousies soon rise to the surface. . . ."

It's a story of two couples who have been good friends, which means that each couple presumes to know the other very well and, of course, that each partner knows their own partner even better. Wrong on all counts!

Gabe (played by Woody Allen), and Judy (played by Mia Farrow), are friends with Jack (played by Sidney Pollack), and Sally (played by Judy Davis). Gabe teaches English at Columbia University in New York City, and Judy has a job at a magazine. Gabe is also a writer, and Judy also writes poetry. Jack is a business man, and Sally works with him.

The Split-Up

The two couples meet at Gabe's and Judy's apartment. All set to all go out for dinner, Jack and Sally, in a very agreeable way, announce to Gabe and Judy that they're splitting up.

This is the pivotal event that sets off the story.

Gabe protests their plan to split and whiningly tries to 'logicalize' it, while Judy becomes distraught. Uh-oh! Why is she so affected, especially to the point of being sick? That's *Clue #1.*

Jack and Sally try to make it a quick discussion and simply indicate that they've been discussing this for some time. Each character in the story is in a relationship, and sooner or later each has private thoughts about attractions to others, but denies it. But Jack and Sally gradually agree that thoughts about others are natural. Of course, Judy denies having such thoughts, (that's *Clue #2*). So does Gabe, but he denies it in an artfully clever stream of consciousness manner—as usual, talking, talking, talking.

However, what they all know, and what all couples know (but almost never talk about), is that the wish for freedom exists universally. At some point in any primary relationship, each partner wishes either for the peaceful disappearance of the other (a thought that is usually immediately dismissed), or, in some cases, the immediate disappearance of the other (peaceful or not). Such thoughts exist even with those couples who never have such a conscious wish—the operative term being "conscious."

These sorts of thoughts occur naturally when little dissatisfactions begin to accumulate. Dissatisfaction is actually anger, and the nature of anger is that it wants to attack, to destroy, to kill, to overall, simply 'get rid of.'

Jack and Sally split. Jack is encouraged by a business associate to phone a well recommended, high-class call girl at $300 dollars a hook-up. Later, Jack tells Gabe that Sally was cold. Prompted by this disclosure, Judy asks Gabe whether he feels she is cold in bed, and also wonders if he's ever attracted to any of his female students.

After the split, Sally finds herself on a date with Paul (played by Timothy Jerome), who has purchased tickets to the opera. Paul's an innocent type who becomes visibly upset when Sally calls Jack while on their date. She emits a string of epithets to, and about, Jack, obviously not concerned about behaving as an hysteric in Paul's presence. Although she professed tranquility about the split-up with Jack, she is obviously very jealous of Jack's very possible dalliances. Needless to say, Paul has gotten more than he bargained for. The upshot is that we see what Jack has been dealing with: Sally is a critical, cynical and dissatisfied person. The underlying meaning of her criticism towards everything and everyone is that she is unconsciously really critical of herself but defends against knowing it by directing her criticality to others. When Paul tells her that the opera is Don Giovanni, Sally cynically answers: "A Don Juan story . . . should cut his dick off."

Relationship Permutations

Woody gives all the couple-permutations a chance alone, scene by scene. So it could be a scene of Gabe and Judy, then Jack and Sally, then Gabe and Jack, then this one with that one and so forth. In this way, we can clearly follow the unfolding of each couple's drama and of each of the four individually.

It's Gabe's turn with Rain. Rain is one of his students and apparently she is a talented writer, an opinion Gabe shares with Judy. Gabe thinks he is treating his interest in Rain with innocense by talking about her talent with Judy. After all, if he was really romantically or sexually interested in Rain, (or for that matter any other woman), why would he talk about her to his wife?

As in every Woody Allen movie where he is the protagonist, he is seen walking in the street with someone, which is when he offers his philosophy. It's a wonderful tradition that Woody has established with respect to this walking and talking device. We see Gabe's playing the innocent with Rain: "I've never cheated." This may be true, but it's also his way of getting his first foothold into the Rain-domain. He refers to himself literally as the innocent moral person, but the underlying message and music, is: 'Here I am honey, get ready!'

And then he lands one of his many one (or two) liners: "I've always had a penchant for Kamikaze women. They crash their plane, but they crash it into you." Apparently this is Woody's warning to himself in the role of Gabe, not to indulge here with this nubile twenty-one year-old — Rain.

Jack is extolling his new girlfriend's attributes to Gabe, this one is named Sam. She's from Delaware, and, in another hilarious throw-away line, adds that her father's in "police work" (a reference to the fact that both Gabe and Jack are really doing something wrong—just about unlawful). Juxtaposing Gabe's and Jack's intellectual and academic cultural life with Sam's background (which is a planet away), he says she's also a fitness and aerobics instructor, that he can relax with her rather than be required to be with Sally's Radcliffe friends.

Suddenly, Judy's ex-husband (played by Benno Schmidt) becomes the narrator and describes Judy as a passive-aggressive person who gets what she wants all the while claiming that she doesn't want much of anything. He says, "Don't let Judy fool you"—(that's *Clue #3)*. The scene goes to Judy who, in a delicious close-up (there are many such exquisitely satisfying close-ups for each of the main characters), responds to the narrator by countering the ex-husband "was impotent; he was totally unromantic." As a counterpunch, the ex-husband, in a comment not meant to be funny but is actually monumentally hilarious, answers Judy's claim that any gift he got her was mechanical and not romantic: "I got her a camera . . . I got her an enlarger for our anniversary." "Enlarger" is Woody's rejoinder in the ex-husband's script, to Judy's "impotent," but in a sense verifies Judy's complaint.

Next, Judy tries to get Sally together with Michael (played by Liam Neeson), who has begun working at the magazine with Judy. Woody knows one should beware of someone pointing you in another's direction because it frequently reveals that the one pointing you in that other's direction is in fact, the one interested in that same object of interest—which in this case means Judy's interest in Michael. And that's *Clue #4*.

Michael indicates he thought Judy was flirting with him. Of course she would deny this, but we are reminded of her ex-husband's words about not letting Judy fool you because apparently Judy gets what Judy wants.

The scene changes and we see Gabe and Rain walking and talking. She wants to know about passion and she asks to read Gabe's novel. In another scene, Jack says defensively about his new girlfriend, Sam, "Okay, she's not Simone de Beauvoir," (uh-oh, trouble, in paradise).

In a scene with Judy, Gabe suddenly decides he wants to have a child with her; in the past, when Judy wanted a child, Gabe refused. Of course his sudden enthusiasm for wanting a child is directly related to his wanting Rain — as far as their age difference is concerned, this makes her the child Gabe really wants.

This is Woody's classic rendition of how acting-out takes place: you want 'A' but rather than fully admitting it to yourself, you rather *do* 'B'. It's *doing* rather than *knowing*. Judy refuses Gabe's suggestion about a child, this is *Clue #5*.

Apparently, whether she knows it or not, Judy's got Michael on her mind.

Judy and Michael continue to incubate their potential relationship by talking about how they're similar with respect to being romantics. Even though Michael still wants to romance Sally, Sally remains critical. For example, Michael and Sally attend a Mahler concert, after which Sally complains about Mahler. What she's really obliquely telling Michael is that he's not the guy, and he's never going to be the guy, but she's doing it indirectly (a bank shot) by referring to Mahler as the ostensible target of her complaint. She's also worried about living alone because a neighbor's house was robbed and she's concerned about robberies and about robbers. Of course, Freud would say that behind the fear is the wish. Dum dee dum dum! So the question is: What is Sally's wish behind her fear of robbers? This is the sort of apprehension and fear that frequently conceals a deeper emotion, one actually connected to a robbery; underneath it all Sally is angry at Jack and at his new relationship that has robbed her of what she really wants—Jack, back! It also means she *wants* the robber to arrive and his name should be—Jack. Overall, Sally is feeling pessimistic about everything and anything, and so she cites the second law of thermodynamics: "Everything turns to shit."

At this point, Gabe and Rain have several events together. As he walks her home they're verbally accosted by her former boyfriend, who was also her shrink. At Rain's 21st birthday party she tells Gabe she's had affairs with older men including her father's partner, her shrink, and her father's friend. (Can Gabe be far behind?). Although Gabe was first ambivalent about showing Rain his novel, he finally relents and gives her the manuscript.

At the birthday party at Rain's apartment, Gabe meets her parents. Gabe, of course is short, and in hilarious contrast, Rain's father is extremely tall—maybe six foot five. In any event, Rain wants to be kissed, and Gabe cautiously complies. He wants to know if she means with both lips and she confirms that it's with both lips. Gabe and Rain kiss passionately as the storm raging outside the penthouse apartment pounds the rooftop and windows. Then, along with the kiss comes an electrifying bolt of lightening—an omen. Gabe, referring to the storm say's it's dangerous (meaning rain—Rain is dangerous to him). The lights that had gone out because of the storm, suddenly come on again, and this moment is the difference between the fantasy of the unlit room, and the reality of the lit one.

Things Are Metamorphosing

In another parallel in the next scene between Judy and Michael, Judy gives Michael her manuscript. They have lunch. It starts to rain. They get wet and run back to the office. Michael takes Judy by surprise by telling her that he loves Sally. Judy says she feels funny (upset) but she's not willing to know that feeling funny is actually anger. And so there's *Clue #6*.

It's obvious that she likes Michael, and wants Michael for herself, and is angry that Michael wants Sally. Judy can't consciously acknowledge any of it.

Next we're at a party attended by Jack and Sam. Jack finds out that Sally is dating and becomes upset (angry) at the news. Sam, totally out of her depth but with an assumption of certainty, is extolling the 'true' virtues of astrology, insisting on its planetary powers to influence earthly inhabitants. Jack is embarrassed and persuasively pushes her out of the party while mumbling under his breath that she's an infant believing in this nonsense about crystals, astrology and soy. Sam says definitely: "They" have proven it. Jack, having had it with Sam in a voice that is mocking and completely derisive, asks who "they" is?

Of course, that's it for Sam! Goodbye.

In a hilarious scene with Michael and Sally in bed having sex, Sally confesses to having obsessive thoughts regarding people who are hedgehogs and those who are foxes, She admits that such rumination distracts her from making love, preventing her from first feeling libidinous, and second, from having an orgasm. In comparing the sophistication levels of Jack and Michael, Sally makes the comment that Michael is deeper than Jack. Of course, this is Woody's humorous aside that does not at all refer to the degree of intelligence and/or erudition of either Jack or

Michael—"deeper" being the operative term. Since obsessive thinking and its partner, rumination, are really the psyche's way of keeping anger repressed, then another hard-core psychological principle is invoked: 'Where there is anger, there is no libido.' This means that so long as Sally doesn't analyze her own underlying anger—the source of her unrelenting criticality—she will never have the personal pleasurable experience of libido, never mind even considering having an orgasm!

Jack, unannounced, enters the house and finds Sally half clothed, and Michael, au naturale. He's incensed that Sally is with another man and tells her he wants to come back. Jack starts making a case for the value of struggle in a relationship and the importance of their joint process of creatively a longtime history together.

In the meantime, Rain has read Gabe's manuscript. She criticizes it, saying it disappoints her insofar as his attitude toward women is shallow. She says she likes the book generally, but with respect to this 'women issue,' she compares it to Leni Riefenstahl's *Triumph of the Will*; the structure and execution is brilliant but the content is horrible. Gabe becomes defensive. Rain realizes that she left the manuscript in a cab, calling it a Freudian slip, and confesses that she's competitive. It's obvious that the Gabe/Rain duo is not to be.

As fate would have it, Sally and Jack, the couple that first split up, are back together and much relieved to have rekindled their relationship, even with all of its disruptions and problems. Speaking of Sam, they commiserate about how long two people can discuss physical fitness and the Zodiak.

Sally announces that Gabe and Judy, who were originally horrified that Sally and Jack were splitting up, have themselves split, and that Judy is now in love with Michael.

Gabe says to his shrink/narrator, "My heart does not know from logic." It's also a reference to when kissing Rain, Gabe says that $50,000 of psychotherapy just went down the drain. In contrast, Michael and Judy have a bad fight and get drenched in the 'rain.' It's the beginning of their romance. Judy is heartbroken because Michael accuses her of being a passive and supportive person as a way of insinuating herself into the feelings of others. That's *Clue #7*. Judy becomes hysterically hurt when Michael profusely apologizes and she falls into his arms.

Now, Sally and Jack are in their warm comfortable bed wrapped around each other. Outside it's storming. She says she's afraid of thunder. He says, "It's a good thing I fixed that leak in the den." It's another of Woody's brilliant connections—a reference to the importance of a solid relationship, one that is able to prevent the 'Rain' from raining-in. To underscore that point, Jack fixed the 'Rain' intrusion—an intrusion that can affect any relationship if the roof isn't rain-proofed. As far as Jack and Sally are concerned, not now, nor ever, will such an intrusion disrupt their lives.

Now, facing the narrator, the clues have all added up and Judy and Michael are together—and they are married. It's Judy's third husband. "I told you she gets what she wants," Judy's first ex-husband says.

Woody Allen on the Psychoanalytic Couch

A book could be written about Woody Allen, solely based on this film. Here, he tells us everything about himself. He is the quintessential disclosure-man. Only his personal self-disclosure is not mundane or typical. He is a bona fide artist of the first order.

Woody fragments himself into chunks, parses himself into components, and then takes each fragment and embeds it, infuses it into the personality of each character of his story. In this way we see the puzzle of Woody Allen in all of the characters. He tells you everything about himself by apportioning all of these fragments of his own identity, and then challenges all of us, first, to notice what he's doing, and second, to put the puzzle together. He has profound insight into each character because each character is some part of him.

Woody is also a virtuoso hipster. He is cool as can be but it's all concealed by his stage persona—that of a skinny-malink "sockee," as he used to say in his stand-up comedy.

And Here Are Woody's Characters

Judy: According to ex-husband number one, she's passive-aggressive, implicitly manipulative, so that despite her whining, she presumably always gets want she wants. This is interesting because psychologically, whining is usually associated with asking for something and before you're even finished asking, you're already expecting a 'No.' So, the whine, even before the request is completely made, is already saying: "Why not—Why can't I have it?" Gabe basically agrees with Judy's claim that she may be "cold." Well, Woody has a part of his personality that is dogged and determined to have it his way, and he also whines when he talks, as though to say, "Well, why not—Why can't I have it?" In addition, despite Woody's apparent adherence to logic and rationality and to the cause and effect of nature (minus any reliance on super-natural explanations), he still succumbs each and every time to what his heart wants. Implicit in this cognitive capitulation to what his heart wants is his single-minded synaptic con-nection to his needs. And this is the personality he assigns to Judy.

Jack: Rattling back and forth, is Jack. He thinks he knows what he wants, but then again he doesn't. When he acts on what he thinks he wants, it eventually peters out, and back he rattles, searching for some meaning he actually may have already had. Like Jack, Woody seems to be in a thrall with Freud's death instinct. Why? The answer lies in an emendation of Freud's death instinct; that is, seeking to reduce all tension to the zero level so that tension is completely eliminated. Jack wants to be free of tension. He finds a young woman who has almost nothing in her head. Brain-dead! But, at least she won't challenge him the way Sally did by always being critical of this or that.

Woody, too, has an element of his personality that seeks zero tension level. Yet, in spite of Woody's search for nirvana (no tension), he writes or produces and directs a film a year, writes stage plays and books, plays improvisational clarinet with a jazz band, and who knows what else. He has an abun-dance of talent combined with an interesting intelligence. But the expression that such talent demands keeps the tension level at close to one hundred percent—just about all of the time. Woody needed someone who would not stand in the way of that magma eruption of genius so he allocates that element of his search for tension-level zero to Jack.

Sally: Sally is hot-wired to be critical. She is Woody's alter ego of nervous energy. She's never satisfied, and is able to find an imperfect needle in any haystack. Woody is also a critical aesthete, however, he has it under wraps. He walks cool, he dresses cool, and he thinks cool. No one 'in the know' would say he's a bundle of nerves vibrating with high-tension visibility or even openly quivering, even though in his humorous persona he actually invites you to see him that way. Woody's high-tension is rather an impatience and a need to conserve all energy so that it's directed to whatever is his project and aim at the moment. Woody flies as does the crow—in a straight line. And yet, if you asked him I bet he will swear to you that he squanders time, perhaps the way Sally squanders time—expending energy in any number of nervous pursuits. But with Woody, the following adage becomes an axiom: If you want a job done, give it to a busy person.

Michael: Here is where Woody's innocence of purpose and honesty—pure as the driven snow—shows up. In a way this aspect of Woody's personality explains why he's so drawn to basketball. In basketball, the guard drives down court looking one way but in a split second, passing the ball the other way. Basketball is a game of angles, bank shots, jump shots from the corner, fakes, alley oops, and the rest. This is exemplified in Woody's approach to Rain. He comes across as a married man who's never cheated on his wife, as a mentor to his students, and as a guru in his novels. He's not quite making a move on Rain, but then again he is, and only as a slight variant of the way Michael does it. Michael is the nice guy with an invisible flirtatious 'whammy' that knocks them dead. Woody, of course, knocks them all dead, making up in a resounding way for what was left undone when he was 14 years old.

Rain: Here is where Woody pins down that aspect of his personality that also turns out to be his nemesis. As Gabe says, he is attracted to women who start off giving him a hard time. This is so, because once rejected, he is brought back to his early history — where it might be reasonably guessed that as an adolescent boy he may have often experienced rejection, or at least did not experience significant success with the objects of his desire. The re-ignition of this memory draws him to a need for conquest like a moth to a flame.

It's also oedipal — hopefully choosing non-challenging young women who will adore him, or at least not be on a level to understand how to critique him. It's libidinal — aiming for it to end up in sex and therefore for him to be the conqueror that wins — especially in the absence of any stated commitment. But the trick is on him, because once they get the real deal, they want to keep it. It also has quite a bit of Brando's Stanley Kowalski in it — take what you want when you want it and how you want it, but do it with Woody Allen stealth; that is, come on like a harmless uncle. And finally, end up not knowing who you are or where you're supposed to be. And that's possibly how Woody feels — he's not sure who he is or where he is — despite the reality of his life where he knows exactly who he is, and exactly where he is.

And the Rest: Here and there, Woody has himself detailed in some of the other characters. In Paul, Woody is showing not merely part of his innocence but also a slice of his belief that he is naïve about how people should be with one another.

In Judy's ex-husband, we get Woody's cynicism born out of a sense of rejection and hypocrisy of the world. In Shawn, the call girl, we get his confidence and know-how in how to handle any exigency. In Richard, Rain's analyst/lover, we see that Woody can be angry and hold a grudge, especially perhaps when he feels 'dissed.' In Sam, Jack's vacuum-packed girlfriend, we see Woody's submerged superstitiousness (especially in sports), despite his overtly committed rationality.

And in the interviewer, we get Woody's mastery regarding what to ask, and that he knows how to pose the salient issue.

The Salient Issue

To Woody Allen the salient issue is that marriage and relationships, and therefore, consistent companionship, is best. This is true despite its ubiquitous attendant difficulties, festering problems, and of course, subsequent life-time deprivations that in all likelihood will obtain within any primary relationship—forever.

Woody's answer is for the partners to talk, talk, and keep talking. For after all, talking is our only choice especially insofar as talking is what really makes us different from lizards or even amoeba. And so, *Husbands and Wives*, is a film that falls in the category of *Duets*, because all of the action and circumstances revolve around what a relationship is and how couples work on their relationships. And Woody is absolutely in favor of couples because he knows that if you don't work on your relationship, the 'rain' will get you.

Woody's range of interests identifies him as a lover of tradition and of culture. In all of his films, he loves to cite literature and art, and of course, his exquisite taste in music is not merely beautiful, it's also healing. Woody knows how to throw and catch a ball very well, and that is highly important to his sky-high 'coolness' index.

And, ah, those close-ups of the characters explaining themselves to the narrator, in which all of these personality characteristics of Woody's emerge, are arguably some of the most fascinating and scrumptious film moments imaginable.

The man who was the architect of *Husbands and Wives*, who either consciously or not engineered this film with Freudian psychoanalytic intent, and beautifully crafted it, deserves to be able to say, "Yes, Gabe, you can go now." In other words, "I've mined all there is to mine," and so, the movie is over. *The End.*

P.S. So, yes, Woody understands it. He understands that on a ten-point scale the best any marriage can be is an eight. And he also knows that eight is high, and that most good marriages in which the partners have gotten a grip on how to struggle with one another, are basically sixes and sevens, and occasionally, and only from time to time, hit eight.

So, perhaps the moral of the story is that it's vital to work out the difficulties with your partner as best you can, even if you must sweep some difficulty under the rug. But remember, talk, talk, talk to your partner, as you sweep.

Chapter 8

THE BRIDGE ON THE RIVER KWAI
(Released, 1957)

From the novel, *The Bridge on the River Kwai*,
by Pierre Boulle
Screenplay by Michael Wilson and Carl Foreman
Produced by Sam Spiegel
Original Music by Malcolm Arnold
Directed by David Lean

Main Cast

William Holden	Shears
Alec Guinness	Colonel Nicholson
Jack Hawkins	Major Warden
Sessue Hayakawa	Colonel Saito
James Donald	Major Clipton
Geoffrey Horne	Lieutenant Joyce
Andre Morell	Colonel Green

Sample Supporting Cast

Peter Williams	Captain Reeves
John Boxer	Major Hughes

Percy Herbert	Grogan
Harold Goodwin	Baker
Ann Sears	Nurse
Heihachiro Okawa	Captain Kanematsu
Keiichiro Katsumoto	Lieutenant Miura
M.R.B. Chakrabandhu	Col. Broom Yai
Vilaiwan Seeboonreaung	Siamese Girl
Ngamta Suphaphongs	Siamese Girl
Javanart Punynchoti	Siamese Girl
Kannikar Dowklee	Siamese Girl

Introduction

It's 1943, the Second World War, and the question is, has the British colonel gone mad? It's a Japanese prison camp in Burma, for crying out loud, and is he actually undertaking the construction of the bridge — for the enemy — so trains carrying Japanese supplies and soldiers connecting Bangkok to Rangoon, can get to their destination more efficiently and quicker? And what about his men, the other British prisoners, why are they, too, working feverishly to complete the bridge on time? Uh-oh, we'd better send some commandos in to blow it up, and never mind the British colonel's motives. But will our own colonel try to stop us despite the fact that we know he is absolutely a loyal and proud British soldier?

So, yes, the British colonel and his men were captured and are now not only imprisoned, but ordered by the Japanese commander of the prison camp, Colonel Saito, to build a bridge in order to facilitate the transportation of Japanese soldiers to their destinations. And the British colonel, Nicholson, is actually doing it. Is Nicholson crazy?

So, it's a story ostensibly about madness. And the question is: What is the possible madness about? Is it about fear, or duplicity, or outright paranoia, or what? Is it about following orders? Is it again another rendition of the problem with the world—to follow orders without thinking, without registering protest? If not that, then what is the nature of the madness that gets the British colonel to lead the charge to build the bridge, and therefore ally himself with his Japanese captor? Because that's what he's doing—essentially allying himself with his Japanese captor.

Trapped

But the real issue is that you're a prisoner on an enemy-held island surrounded by hundreds of miles of ocean and dense jungle. In such a case one must work and to do what one is told, and at the same time, try and survive. Apparently, there is no escape. This is a story about the vicissitudes, the ins and outs of a circumstance, where one finds oneself in an extreme condition of helplessness. The question becomes, what happens to your personality—does it change, or does it become even more rigid under such disempowering conditions? To top it all off, remember it's happening to you in the sweltering heat of an island, somewhere in Asia—a place that's not terribly close to home—that is, to London.

You are trapped!

The Main Story

The DVD encapsulates the story this way:

> "When British P.O.W.s build a vital railway
> bridge in enemy-occupied Burma, Allied com-
> mandos are assigned to destroy it. . . ."

Colonel Nicholson (played by Alec Guinness) has a problem. The problem isn't that he's on an island in the far Pacific,
in a Japanese prison camp; no, the problem is that he will not
abide by the edict issued by the Japanese commander of the
prison camp that requires all of the British prisoners (as well
as the lone American, Shears, played by William Holden), to
work on the construction of the bridge over the river Kwai. This
is the bridge that will more efficiently facilitate transportation
of goods and Japanese soldiers to their destinations rather
than requiring them to be transported on much longer jour-
neys. However, Col. Nicholson insists that the prisoners will not
work if their officers are not granted solely administrative du-
ties. Nicholson goes by the book, the one containing the rules
of the Geneva Convention regarding prisoners and rank, which
specifically states that officers should not do manual labor.

The Japanese head of the prison camp is the brutal Colonel Saito (played by Sessue Hayakawa). Col. Saito will have
none of it, and to make the point, slaps Nicholson across the
face with the aforementioned Geneva Convention rule-book,
drawing blood. Nicholson, courageous and unwavering, is not
fazed. He maintains his composure and bearing as he faces
the glaring Saito in the open, sandy, arid field of the main prison compound.

Col. Nicholson emerges as a stalwart soldier who will not yield to Saito. As punishment, Saito has Nicholson put in the "oven," a square ramshackle shack made of wood and metal, that "bakes" in the scorching sun. The oven is too small for the prisoner to stretch out, and he will not be given any drinking water. Saito means business.

But Nicholson won't budge an inch!

And then there is Shears, the American, who wants to escape. Americans are, after all, entrepreneurial.

Shears is a grave digger in the prison cemetery. From this point of view, it becomes clear that all the British prisoners, himself included, will end up quite dead in this cemetery sooner or later.

Shears sees Saito as dehumanized, but Nicholson believes that Saito can be reasonable even though he also refers to Saito as "mad." Nicholson's opinion is partially validated when Saito tells Nicholson that he will count to three. If Nicholson does not yield regarding his officers working alongside the other prisoners, he will be shot. A truck backs up directly at Nicholson, and in the back of the truck sit some Japanese soldiers at the ready, manning a machine gun. Saito begins his count but is interrupted by the British Major Clipton (played by James Donald). Clipton persuades Saito to reconsider, arguing that the shooting of Nicholson and the other officers would be witnessed by many of the prisoners. He further shames Saito by referring to the cowardly act of shooting unarmed men—especially after Saito had just chastised Nicholson and the other officers by claiming that their surrender to the Japanese was in itself cowardly and disgraceful.

Saito reconsiders. Instead of killing Nicholson, he decides to break him by cooking him in the oven, and by incarcerating the other officers with similar deprivation. Nicholson resists and it becomes clear to Saito that Nicholson will die rather than capitulate. This is a problem for Saito because the bridge has been ordered to be completed by a certain date and if not, Saito will feel shamed and obligated by Japanese tradition to migrate to the great prison-camp in the sky.

"Madness"

From his perspective, Saito thinks Nicholson is (as Nicholson has thought of Saito) quite mad. Shears thinks they're all nuts especially for accepting the assumption that there's no escape. And Clipton, at the story's end says it for everyone: "Madness, madness!"

Saito declares that an attempt to escape the island is "an escape from reality." He unquestioningly believes it is impossible to escape. Shears has other plans; he kills one of the guards and, with his God-given guile and his American determination, slips into the jungle. He barely makes it to some poor village where the inhabitants, apparently hostile to the Japanese, help him. He then sets out to sea on a raft and by pure luck is spotted and rescued by sea plane.

But is it madness when Saito eventually releases Nicholson and capitulates to his demand that his officers not work along with the enlisted men? Is that Saito's madness? Or, is it more Saito's madness that he abandons his position of absolute strength and surrenders his will to a completely disempowered prisoner, and in doing so, experiences his own shame in the impending capitulation. Saito, alone in his command hut, is beside himself with fury, weeping at his own defeat in the struggle of wills between him and Nicholson.

The Bridge

Now comes the surprise. In consultation with his British prisoner/engineers, Nicholson learns of a problem in the location where Saito wants to build the bridge, and where now Nicholson's men are daily sabotaging the ongoing construction. Apparently the ground under the water will never be able to stand the weight of the bridge or anything on it. Therefore, isn't it good that the bridge will collapse as the train traverses it?

No, as a matter of fact, that's not good. According to Nicholson, they need to find a better place to build the bridge so that the structure of the bridge will be perfectly stable and functional—to really make it a solid, good bridge, one befitting the expertise and sophistication of British superiority exemplified in all culturally civilized respects.

So they do it. They find the right spot some hundred yards downstream and begin. Nicholson is confident that his men can build the bridge, and his men do it with the contagion of Nicholson's verve, excitement, and motivation in getting the job done the right way—the British way!

Clipton says Nicholson's position about what has to be done could be considered treason. It would be obvious collaboration with the enemy. Nicholson offers an idiosyncratic response that begins to reveal that his thinking is highly personalized and even skewed. He says: "People will remember who built it."

Commandos

Shears has made it to Ceylon. There he reunites with his wife, and feels that his war days are essentially over. Enter

British Major Warden (played by Jack Hawkins). Warden has gotten reconnaissance information that the bridge is being built, and it's now his job to blow it to smithereens. He forms a commando unit that will be parachuted onto the island with the express purpose of blowing up the sucker.

He is aware that Shears is familiar with the terrain and knows the direction to the prison camp but his attempts to enlist Shears to join his commandos are declined. However, Warden has gotten the army dossier on Shears. It reveals that Shears, in a situation to save his life, took a dead soldier's identity, a punishable offense according to army code. It is heavily hinted that the army could 'forget' the incident, if Shears agrees to join Major Warden's commando unit.

Shears has no choice, and in they go. In the meantime, Nicholson and his officers are guiding the construction of the bridge. Nicholson informs Saito that unless the Japanese soldiers help in the construction, there is no possibility that the bridge will be finished on time. Saito complies and the beautiful bridge actually gets beautifully built.

Meanwhile, Warden, Shears, and the other commandos, along with a male guide and several female guides from the Island village, get to the bridge. They receive a message indicating when the train is due and they decide to blow up the bridge exactly as the train is racing across it.

At the finish, Nicholson is slowly and quietly walking across his completed bridge, admiring his work, caressing and loving its beautiful carriage, and proud bearing. Simultaneously, the commandos, under the light of the moon, swim beneath the bridge and begin stringing dynamite charges. They unfurl cable leading from the dynamite charges under the bridge to a spot down river where they can be concealed from view. They will await the train and at the right moment, push that dynamite plunger.

The Train

It's the next day and the train is relentlessly approaching. Saito joins Nicholson on the bridge but their reverie is interrupted when Nicholson notices the cable wire under the bridge running down stream. Apparently, the river has receded during the night so that its sandy bottom is exposed in some areas. The commandos now see the same thing.

Nicholson and Saito descend to the river's edge and begin to wade in the water. Nicholson sees it all and knows the implication. In an urgent and pleading voice Shears says out loud to himself but also loud enough so that the other commandos can hear him—"Kill him! Kill him!" Shears knows that Nicholson must be erased. The battle begins and shots are fired. The commando, Lieutenant Joyce (played by Geoffrey Horne), who is concealed behind a boulder with his hand ready to detonate the dynamite, is shot and killed. The train is almost on the bridge. Shears, in an American moment, jumps out and rushes toward the action in order to salvage the deal, and to kill Nicholson in good measure. Shears, is himself shot—and killed.

The train is on the bridge. At that instant, Nicholson has a moment of clarity and finally truly understands the implications of his behavior. As he is shot, he says: "What have I done?" and he falls on the detonator, thereby blowing the bridge to kingdom-come, as the locomotive and all its cars plunge into the river.

Along with the destruction of the bridge and trains, Nicholson, Saito, Shears, Joyce, some Japanese soldiers, and the villager guide are all dead. Warden and the female villager guides survive. They see it all from a high ridge overlooking the river.

Clipton also sees it from a wide vantage point and says:

"Madness, madness, madness."

Colonel Nicholson on the Couch

It's a relationship story between Col. Nicholson and Col. Saito, and this is the central fact that places the story in the category of *Duets*. Col. Saito is the apparent dominant captor, while Col. Nicholson is, under such conditions, obviously the submissive partner.

This sort of relationship can be compared to a marriage in which the dominant partner rescues a seemingly forlorn or weak one. Usually it's the man rescuing the woman and he completes the rescue by marrying her. It's this way because gender difference in opportunity usually has favored men and ignored women (often the man has had the career and money). In the case of Nicholson and Saito, an analogy can be drawn; in an exaggerated way, their so-called marriage is one of master and slave. The Saito-Nicholson relationship is a situation where one is in control and the other not; one is dominant and the other is ostensibly submissive.

A Psychological Dynamic

As is often the case with such intersections of people (marriages), the dominant one gradually becomes the recessive one, while the one who was rescued and originally expected to be submissive, eventually becomes dominant. A typical side effect of this reversal is that the formerly submissive one who is now dominant, usually becomes only concerned with personal needs and therefore, can completely ignore the presumed given entitlements of the formerly dominant one.

When this happens in a marriage, a kind of sado-masochistic pattern emerges in which now the 'new' dominant one (frequently the wife), becomes almost immune to any affectionate interest in her partner, and withdraws from sexual contact. The former dominant one is now in a state of deprivation and cannot elicit even a smidgeon of concern from the now dominant wife.

How is it possible that such a reversal of fortune for the originally dominant partner can occur? What is this phenomenon all about? To begin with we must realize that personality may be the hardest, most solid and inflexible substance in existence. It is also true that one's personality configuration composed in part of needs, traits, attitudes, impulses, emotions, and predilections, relentlessly resists pressures to change. Here and there, and based upon all sorts of experiences, certain changes can be achieved, but many changes will usually be contoured by the personality to fit into its program of needs, so that the change does not cause trouble and is seamlessly assimilated.

In the present duet of Nicholson and Saito, Nicholson is initially the putative, recessive one and Saito, his captor, is initial the technically dominant one. Saito insists on Nicholson's obedience and compliance, and because of the dominance/submission circumstance in which they both find themselves, Saito expects that his assumption will be automatically satisfied. In marriages that have this same kind of initial pattern between the partners, the rescuer/dominant one is attracted to the actual rescue itself because of a basic assumption—that the rescued party will never offer significant resistance to demands made by the rescuer, and further, will be grateful to have survived so well by virtue of the rescuer's good graces.

Nonsense! The rescued/presumed submissive one needs to be rescued in the first place because of deeply etched personality traits that resisted all sorts of demands from the world to adapt, to change, to grow, to be flexible. Such a person, for whatever reason(s), could not, and therefore would not change and would not adapt. The end result is that this sort of person is usually spectacularly stubborn; they are in a state of absolute resistance to change. They experience anxiety only by the demands made on them from the outside world, an underlying anger at anyone making such demands (especially at the dominant rescuer). They value pride above all things, the only thing they think they have—their own inviolability!

"You can't compel me to do anything that contradicts or goes against my grain," is this person's creed.

Enter, Col. Nicholson.

The Key to Nicholson's Personality

This business of resisting any kind of outside pressure that goes against his grain—his creed—is what precisely turns the situation between Nicholson and Saito around. Nicholson's pride in his relinquishment of all worldly goods, and rather in his complete focus and loyalty to his profession as a soldier, will not tolerate any external force that tries to alter this soldier's agenda. No matter what Saito does to him, Nicholson won't budge. Saito, under pressure to build the bridge, begins to capitulate, and we see the transformation of his dominance into irrelevance, and simultaneously we also see Nicholson's recessive, ostensible submissive position (by virtue of his prisoner status) gain the absolute ascendancy so that his new empowerment now contrasts with Saito's new disempowerment.

Additionally, we can see that what Nicholson considers his ultimate loyalty to the British army is a subterfuge, even a self-delusion; yes, Nicholson consciously and apparently behaves as though he would die for his country and do its bidding for the sake of country, but unconsciously, and actually, he's only interested in his own needs. True to form, just as the recessive partner is assumed to be grateful and therefore interested in the dominant one, the recessive one does what recessives always do—they take over, and dismiss the partner.

So, Saito, be careful of dominance-submission assumptions. First take the measure of your captive's pride-index. Since that captive is in a terribly disempowered initial position, you would do well to be sure that underneath all of his agony as a prisoner, as a submissive disempowered one, he is very definitely enraged. His fury, based upon the humiliation to his pride—which is equivalent to his sense of his very being, of who he is—will then have the potential to take you down—down to dust.

The Underlying Meaning

Nicholson is an army man with conscious and clear ideas of his duty as a soldier, which supposedly supersedes his personal needs. When push comes to shove however, his conscious and clear idea of duty pales in favor of his own personal unconscious agenda which has nothing at all to do with what he thought was always conscious and clear.

The point is we don't always know who we are. In Nicholson's case, his utter disempowerment was ultimately translated into an empowered triumph. He loves the image of the envisioned bridge anthropomorphized as a bridge with proud bearing. It's not a coincidence that his love of this "bridge of proud bearing" resembles his own comportment as a proud soldier of the British army. Therefore, the bridge is him—he had it constructed in his own image: strong, willful, clean, proud, and, sturdy. This bridge will stand the test of time.

In another glimpse of his madness, Nicholson has a plaque made indicating that the bridge was the handiwork of soldiers of the British army and in an abbreviated dedication ceremony has the plaque fastened to a beam on the bridge. His thinking has been contaminated by his inner life, by a particular inner impulse. Part of this craziness is what is called 'tangential thinking.' It's the kind of thinking that emanates solely from the logic of personal needs minus any input from external reality. He even goes so far as to tangentially say: "People will remember who built it." In other words, he's off on his personal logic of needing adulation for a job well done and does not even consider the actual crossover he's made—British officer to enemy conspirator. Again, his vision of the bridge is simply an externalization of how he sees his own image.

On top, Nicholson, is a dedicated, and sacrificial object to his creed and his cause, but underneath, he is a narcissist. He is only concerned with the vision and reflection of his own beauty, his singular stoic carriage, and his absolute rigidity of what he considers correctness. On the surface his creed is honor and country; underneath his real creed is — self.

The question is: What drives the narcissism and assures such narcissism its success? The answer is that it is Nicholson's obsessive rumination regarding how that bridge can and should be beautiful, and then his compulsive drive to achieve that exact picture in his mind when the beautiful bridge is completed — beautifully.

It is because of this narcissism that Nicholson can veer off the beaten path and find himself skewed into an alternate reality. That is really the basis of his madness. He is now operating solely with his inner narcissistic signal that also needs an external rationale for the goal of that narcissism to be successfully realized.

Average narcissism — even clinical narcissism — is not considered psychotic. Under the pressured conditions of a brutal prison camp, where one is rendered helpless, almost any underlying personality pattern can be pushed over the line to its psychotic extent. Since this dynamic is conditional, once the aggrieved condition is somehow lifted, the psychosis can abate and the person can then understand the contrast between their psychotic narcissistic behavior (building the bridge in his own image), in comparison to their usual normal self (being a loyal and good soldier). That's what seems to have happened to Colonel Nicholson.

So the answer to Major Clipton, as he surveys the devastated landscape of bridge, bodies, and train, and repeatedly intones, "madness," is the proposition that yes, it is madness. Because Nicholson, in his insistence that he's loyal solely to duty and country, actually proves that's not the point that truly motivates him. What really informs and motivates Nicholson is the narcissistic composition of his psyche—and nothing else! Given the pressure he was under, his psyche, in its unconscious organization of narcissistic needs and associated impulses, proved to be stronger than all other considerations of his life. His personal empowerment through the building of the bridge emerged triumphantly because of his alternate narcissistically psychotic guise.

His narcissistic peak moment occurs after the bridge had been beautifully constructed; he walks across it, looking at it, touching it, and reveling in it. It is the perfect reflection of his self-image—a beautiful phallic one. The bridge is his phallus, his ego and his narcissism. When he looks over the bridge, he's really looking into the beautiful future, and when he looks down at the river, he is first and foremost looking for his image in the water. Talk about classic narcissism! It is a classic narcissistic attachment to success by an individual who exists in an alternate persona in which he delights in his oceanic illusion—actually a delusion of omnipotence and grandiosity.

The need for recognition and acknowldgment of superiority, for impulses that aim directly toward self-aggrandizement, conceal an individual's profound sense of inferiority, imperfection, and immaturity. The narcissism is a monumental compensatory cloak that covers the entire personality.

What Keeps the Narcissism Fixed and in Place?

Now we arrive at the personality mechanisms that are the nuts and bolts designed to keep Nicholson's narcissism fixed and in place. Here we are considering what are known as the so-called anal traits of obsessional and compulsive personality mechanisms. Nicholson shows these qualities in bold relief. First of all, Nicholson's 'orderliness' (in his need to organize his men), 'obstinacy' (Saito knows that Nicholson must have it his own way or he won't do anything), and 'parsimony' (Nicholson will build the bridge in the most efficient way possible) comprise what is psychoanalytically known as "the anal triad." Along with this triad we also see that Nicholson operates with strong needs for control, perfectionism, righteousness, rigidity, objectification, rigid high expectations, and a strong need for closure. It is an obsessive and compulsive tyranny, all of which service his narcissistic needs.

Perhaps the moral of the story is that to be resilient in life, to retain one's normalcy, one needs to look past his own self-interest. More importantly, one needs to keep a focus on others, on the real world, and always be on guard about keeping oneself from becoming overly insular.

The End

Nicholson's last words, as he regains a momentary grip on reality—precisely when he's about to fall on the dynamite plunger that will blow up the bridge—are: "What have I done?"

And so, even in his moment of clarity—his very last moment before he dies—the operative term in Nicholson's last utterance is: "I."

But finally, it is an "I" focused on the real world.

Chapter 9

PRETTY WOMAN
(Released, 1990)

Screenplay by J.F. Lawton
Produced by Arnon Milchan / Steven Reuther
Executive Producer, Laura Ziskin
Co-producer: Gary W. Goldstein
Associate Producer: Walter von Huene
Original Music by James Newton Howard
Directed by Gary Marshall

Main Cast

Richard Gere	Edward Lewis
Julia Roberts	Vivian Ward
Jason Alexander	Philip Stuckey
Hector Elizondo	Barney Thompson
Ralph Bellamy	James Morse
Laura San Giacomo	Kit De Luca
Alex Hyde-White	David Morse
Patrick Richwood	Night Elevator Operator, Dennis

Sample Supporting Cast

Elinor Donahue	Bridget
R. Darrell Hunter	Darryl The Limo Driver
Larry Miller	Mr. Hollister
Dey Young	Snobby Saleswoman
Abdul Salaam El Razzac	Happy Man
Amy Yasbeck	Elizabeth Stuckey
Judith Baldwin	Susan
Larry Hankin	Landlord
Kathleen Marshall	Day Desk Clerk
Marvin Braverman	Room Service Waiter
Rodney Kageyama	Japanese Businessman
Shane Ross	Marie
Michael French	Maitre D'
Stacy Keach Sr.	Senator Adams
Lucinda Crosby	Olsen Sister
Nancy Locke	Olsen Sister
Karin Calabro	Violetta in "La Traviata"
Bruce Eckstut	Alfredo in "La Traviata"

Introduction

Welcome to Hollywood. What's your dream? Some come true, some don't but according to this story, only one question needs to be answered: Do you have a growth arc or not? The audience follows to see if you ascend or descend, succeed or fail. If you ascend up the ladder, your dream comes true; if you descend down the ladder, your dreams fail. It's fascinating to observe this ongoing process. After all is said and done, it's Hollywood where happy endings are anticipated and, unlike real life, dreams very often do come true. Therefore, who knows when lightening will strike?

And that's how this movie begins; a guy meets a gal in quite a random fashion; they're from hugely opposite worlds. Nevertheless, they have much in common, fall in love, and each, by virtue of the unfolding of their relationship, cures the other's respective neurosis.

How Edward and Vivian Influence One Another

So the question becomes how does the stunning, beautiful Vivian Ward (played by Julia Roberts), a down and out hooker with no visible upward-mobility prospects, mix with stupendously wealthy, very handsome Edward Lewis (played by Richard Gere), a high finance, corporate-raider type? Like oil and water which cannot mix unless an emulsifying agent is added, if we just add soap to the oil and water and shake it up, an almost magical transformation occurs.

With Vivian and Edward, the soap is the gradual melding of a relationship with all of its permutations. First you put all of Edward's attitudes, likes and dislikes, into the pot along with Vivian's personal baggage. The contents of the pot begin to simmer, and then rise to a high flame, and everything really starts to cook. In other words, just add their respective personalities onto the physical attraction of the relationship and shake it up.

Edward, in a very calm and uncritical way, teaches Vivian to be more of a lady, someone with a bit more decorum and grace. Correspondingly, Vivian helps Edward become more of a 'mentsh.' The question is: How does this occur with each of them? With Edward, it's his generosity of spirit, his love for the finer things of life—both tangible and intangible—that influences Vivian. With Vivian, it's her overall integrity that becomes compelling for Edward. Surprise—the heartless corporate-raider is generous of spirit and the opportunistic hooker has integrity. In both cases, these attributes—generosity of spirit, on the one hand, and integrity on the other—are contagious, and of course, immensely persuasive.

This is a fabulous Cinderella love story that has romance, a frequent display of rhapsodic events, and Hollywood dream-fulfillment that is portrayed as the realization of a wonderful wished-for fantasy.

The Main Story

The DVD describes the story this way:

> "When successful corporate mogul Edward Lewis meets independent and carefree Vivian Ward their two lives are worlds apart. But Vivian's energetic spirit challenges Edward's no-nonsense, business-minded approach to life, sparking an immediate attraction. He teaches her about the finer things in life; she teaches him that love could be the best investment he ever made."

Edward Lewis is at a party having a difficult phone conversation with his girlfriend. During the conversation, they decide to break up. Fed up, he borrows his lawyer's gorgeous Lotus automobile and takes off. Driving in this 'Batmobile' through a seedy area of Los Angeles, he gets lost and he stops at a curbside completely unaware that he is in Hollywood's under-belly, populated by prostitutes, hustlers, pimps, and the home-less. Edward is simply looking to ask someone for directions.

Enter, Vivian Ward. She approaches the car with an appar-ent 'John' behind the wheel. She begins her repartee; while Edward is trying to get a handle on geography, Vivian is plying her trade. Before you know it, she's in the car and as it turns out, she can drive it better than he can. Of course she's wear-ing an outlandish hooker's outfit including high black boots and a short midriff. For sure, in the race for 'gorgeous,' the Lotus comes in second.

She asks for some token money for giving him directions and he agrees. When she pulls up at his plush Beverly Hills hotel, Edward gives her cab money to get back to where she started. She takes the cab money, but rather than hail a cab, she waits for a bus. Edward feels something toward her and invites her to stay with him. Edward is so affluent, so accus-tomed to getting whatever it is he wants, that having a woman of the night accompany him into this perfectly staid, palatial hotel, doesn't bother him at all.

They Begin to Talk

They arrive at Edward's penthouse suite and from that moment on throughout the story, all of their character contrasts emerge. He is a business man extraordinaire who cannibalizes down-and-out companies. He buys them and sells off pieces for sizeable profit. Similarly, she is in her business strictly for the money and is able to detach from any emotion regarding her work. He too, is detached from any of his behavior as a 'cannibal' because when he takes over a company and does his deed, many people find themselves out of work. At one point Edward even crudely says: "You and I are such similar creatures . . . we both screw people for money." Although they're both in it for the money, and although they have an uninterrupted repartee throughout, they never really joke about money.

He reveals that he has an ex-wife, and now an ex-girlfriend, and is basically afraid of heights (acrophobic). Still he always rents this penthouse with an outdoor terrace overlooking the city because it's just the best one can have. He'll never settle for anything but the best (a veiled nod to their impending developing relationship).

With his classic acrophobic symptom, he hardly ever goes out on the terrace. She reveals that no matter who she's with, kissing on the mouth is taboo. She understands the truism that in sex, saying "I love you" is usually only episodic and originates in the groin, while kissing on the mouth says "I love you" straight from the heart.

Edward is so taken with this beautiful, charming, intelligent, sincere Vivian that he negotiates a week-long stay for $3,000 dollars (a discount based loosely on Vivian's claim that she earns $300 an hour). As Vivian will be accompanying Edward on trips, and for dinners, she needs to shop for clothes. Edward provides the cash and off Vivian goes to Rodeo Drive, a place that her hooker roommate Kit (played by Laura San Giacomo), tells her is *the* place to shop in Beverly Hills. Dressed in the same clothes she was wearing when she met Edward, the saleswomen see what she is, and in no uncertain terms, she is given her walking-papers right out of the shop. She returns to the hotel befuddled, only to be confronted by the Manager, Mr. Barney Thompson (played by Hector Elizondo). At first he lets her know she's basically not wanted in his hotel, but then because of Vivian's sincere disclosure of her dilemma, he calls Bridget, a saleswoman he knows (played by Elinor Donahue). Vivian arrives at the shop and Bridget, a kindred human, decks her out.

Edward's Goose is Cooked

When Edward sees Vivian in the dress she got at Bridget's he flips out. Vivian has become an exquisite, ethereal vision. He says she is "stunning." Without a doubt, this man has taste! And now, the romance is etched. Everyone can see it and everyone can feel it—gorgeous Julia Roberts arm-in-arm with handsome Richard Gere, obviously and naturally, walking into the future.

Edward brings Vivian to dinner with Mr. James Morse (played by Ralph Bellamy), and Morse's grandson (played by Alex Hyde-White). Morse is a wise elder statesman/business-man/industrialist whose company is in dire straits and is in line to be gobbled up by Edward's company. Morse decides not to go down without a fight. In the meantime, Vivian is having trouble knowing what to do with the escargot.

Edward and Vivian are becoming ever closer and they begin to confide in one another. She's a wayward child, and declares that when people put you down, you start to believe it. Edward shares that he'd been on the 'outs' with his father and hadn't seen him for more than fourteen years. He had not even attended his father's funeral. Edward says, "I was very angry with him," adding that it cost him $10,000 in therapy to say that. He tells her that his father left his mother for another woman and took all of his money with him, leaving the family to fend for itself. But then he offers a coda to the story by regaling Vivian with the information that he eventually bought and sold his father's company, decimating it piece by piece.

In addition to these intimacies, there's a scene where Vivian sees that Edward is an accomplished pianist. Of course they've now been having sex—without kissing on the mouth—but despite that, Vivian is falling in love. At one point while Edward is dozing in a chair, she leans over and kisses him on the mouth. He opens his eyes and kisses her back. Later in the story Edward is sleeping but has his arms around her as she says in a kind of whisper to herself: "I love you."

When Vivian tells Edward about how difficult it was to shop, he accompanies her on a wild shopping spree. Of course, with Edward along to grease the skids, Vivian is now decked to the gills.

Edward Becomes Immunized Against the Poison

Enter, Philip Stuckey (played by Jason Alexander), the stereotypical blood sucker. As Edward's lawyer, Stuckey does all the dirty work in setting up the kill of the company and cannibalizing it. Stuckey loves the hunt, especially kicking them when they're down. He even makes a play for Vivian after Edward stupidly confides to him that Vivian is a hooker. Seeing Vivian as a paid-for-pleasure companion while they are all at a polo match, Stuckey is rude to Vivian. Later in the story he actually tries to sexually attack her. Edward arrives and knocks him down.

Stuckey is now out of Edward's life and remains his dehumanized self, while Edward, as a result of being with Vivian, is becoming humanized and far less cynical. He is beginning to literally and figuratively feel the grass under his feet. At one point the emerging 'new Edward' says to Stuckey: "We don't build anything Phil. We don't make anything." That's where the bell started to toll for Stuckey. Before they were peas in a pod, but after Stuckey made a move on Vivian, he remains the only pea in the pod. Under Vivian's influence, Edward has now become immunized against the poison that had been contaminating his soul.

The romance is almost sealed when on a trip to San Francisco in Edward's private jet, he tells Vivian that when experiencing opera, crying is a sign of feeling human. When Vivian and Edward are seated in the best box at the opera, being true to herself, she looks over the banister and quickly comments: "Where's the band?" And that's Vivian, giving air time to whatever she's thinking in the most unselfconscious way. Edward is charmed by it despite its impoverished informational implication.

Of course, Vivian cries at the opera. Of course, Edward sees it. Now it's getting serious. Edward decides to partner with Mr. Morse instead of defeating him. He likes Morse because he was concerned about his employees. When Morse finally is willing to sell, he tells Edward that he will but Edward must make allowances for Morse's loyal employees. Edward does him one better by joining forces with Morse and in very moving moment, Morse says to Edward:

"I'm proud of you."

Vivian has done it. Edward Lewis is now a mentsch. But, one more little bit of unfinished business is still on the table. Edward wants to keep Vivian in an apartment. Vivian is insulted and refuses. Her rectitude was demonstrated earlier in the film when they had a bad argument and rather than take the $3,000 dollars—she took her clothes and bolted. Edward apologized and got her somewhat reluctantly to return. But again, she will not compromise her dignity, and so she leaves and returns to the apartment she had shared wit Kit.

Vivian is now leaving Los Angeles. She plans on finishing high school and starting a new life. Edward is told by Mr. Thompson of the hotel that Vivian was driven home by Darryl the limo driver (played by R. Darrell Hunter). Edward sees daylight and has Darryl take him to Vivian's apartment. Bags all packed, as Vivian is about to leave, when she hears a car horn blowing. She goes to the window and there is Edward standing up through the sunroof of the limo, waving at her with flowers in his hands.

Edward begins climbing up the fire escape to the top floor as Vivian begins climbing down. He's overcoming his acrophobia.

And that's it, folks.

Edward Lewis on the Couch

Well, that's really not entirely it. The film starts with a message vocalized by a seemingly somewhat down-on-his luck, tall lanky African-American who is walking across a street proclaiming: "Welcome to Hollywood. What's your dream? Some come true, some don't."

While Edward didn't have a dream, Vivian had one but it was fantasy-land. She didn't stand a chance of having her dream come true until some Lotus fortuitously entered her life. The real charm that produced Edward's miracle was the same fortuitous event. It was the advent of Vivian Ward in Edward

Lewis's life. The prostitute for profit met the profiteer, and the duet they played was a beautiful one.

What was it in this story that nurtured Edward's growth-arc containing the most important growth experience of his life. Of course it was meeting Vivian. But that's not all of it. Vivian warmed him up—enabled his heart to feel loved, and also for his heart to love. She helped morph him from a cynical, habitual exploiter into a concerned human being. Her implied mantra was that one can be productive and rich and still be human, as easily as one can become rich by practicing institutional dissections, as Edward had been doing all along.

'If You Spot It, You Got It'

It also needs to be remembered that Edward was terribly angry at his father. However, what Edward never realized was—like father, like son. Edward had incorporated a typical way of "being" directly from his cold and objectively nasty father. And so Edward did exactly what his father had done—he destroyed families, in the transformational guise of destroying companies. Edward was imitating being the "bad father." This is known in psychoanalytic understanding as internalizing same gender identification and also known in the social psychological arena as "identification with the aggressor." In popular culture, we also attribute such identification with the aggressor as imitation as well as the internalization of a father's image into one's own unconscious sense of self. It's a clear psychological projection; that is, such identification can be seen in the aphorism –'if you spot it, you got it.'

Without Edward being able to work through his hatred and anger toward his father, he would most likely, never be free of being like his father. His relationship with Vivian, although important in warming him up, would also not be able to help him fully through his dilemma. No. What Edward needed was to meet a good father-figure and have a relationship with that person. It's what is known psychoanalytically as having a positive transference. It lays the ground for one's unconscious troubling stuff to be worked on, worked out, and worked through.

Therefore, Edward's conversion from trying to kill and dismember Morse's company, to joining forces and working together with him was the touchstone of Edward's transformation. The most derivative dividend for him was that he was able to commit to Vivian and, in fact, ran to get her back.

The Edward/Morse connection was the good father transference—the antibiotic—that knocked out the anger/hatred bacterial infection that was festering in Edward's psychological inner life. This new relationship also enabled Edward to overcome his acrophobia. The horrible prospect of reaching toward his real father (which when Edward was a boy, meant reaching up high), was the basis of his acrophobia; it became the symbolic equivalent of Edward's resistance to being on that higher ground that he saw his father inhabiting. So, yes, he expressed it by avoiding heights.

Now, with this new good father in his life—no more acrophobia. Now Edward can go as high as he wants—and up the fire escape he goes. The killing of companies was always his way of living "down low," and not "up high." With Vivian and his good father, he can now climb as high as he wants—sky's the limit!

At the end of the story when Edward takes the limo and sets out to get Vivian back, the limo driver blows the horn, Vivian goes to the window, they see one another, Edward gets out of the limo and climbs up the fire escape to where Vivian is waiting, and that's—amore!

The moral of the story of love conquering all, gets help when accompanied by the opportunity to understand and work out whatever conflicts bind you.

So, welcome to Hollywood. Some dreams come true, and some don't.

For Edward and Vivian they came true.

Chapter 10

THE WAY WE WERE
(Released, 1973)

Screenplay by Arthur Laurents
Produced by Ray Stark
Associate Producer, Richard A. Roth
Original Music, Marvin Hamlisch
Directed by Sidney Pollack

Main Cast

Barbra Streisand	Katie Morosky
Robert Redford	Hubbell Gardiner
Bradford Dillman	J .J.
James Woods	Frankie McVeigh
Lois Chiles	Carol Ann
Patrick O'Neal	George Bissinger
Viveca Lindfors	Paula Reisner

Sample Supporting Cast

Allyn Ann McLerie	Rhea Edwards
Murray Hamilton	Brooks Carpenter

Herb Edelman	Bill Verso
Diana Ewing	Vicki Bissinger
Sally Kirkland	Pony Dunbar
Susan Blakely	Judianne
Brendan Kelly	Rally Speaker

Introduction

It's a college campus in 1937. Katie Morosky (played by Barbra Streisand) is the campus radical who supports the Soviet Union's fight against Franco's putsch to take over Spain. She's also a member of the Communist Youth League, a champion of civil rights, and considers herself an American patriot who is passionately for liberty and equality. She's Jewish, highly intelligent, and very serious. Her problem is that her outrage at injustice unfailingly trumps her inability to keep her mouth shut!

In her unrelenting and strident march toward her view of the right thing to do, she ultimately loses Hubbell Gardiner, the love of her life (played by Robert Redford). Katie just can't hold it back; she's got to express every smidgeon of righteous indignation—and she'll do it impulsively whenever she feels it, whether or not it's socially appropriate, without any concern for her own best interest. Katie is only interested in things being fair. It would be difficult to accuse Katie of being even gratuitously fun-loving. Almost to a fault, Katie is always sober, usually replacing humor with cynicism. The exception is when it comes to Hubbell Gardiner, because she's just about always drunk with love for him—this blonde super-popular definitely N. J. (not Jewish) campus hero.

At her well-attended peace rally, Katie sees the potential for greatness in the student body at the college. She also sees that many of the students often behave superficially and are fun-loving to a fault. Hubbell seems intimately connected to these shallow fun-loving students.

Hubbell is the guy who does everything well, is an extremely talented writer (which Katie is not), and is extraordinarily good looking. Even though most of the students treat Katie derisively—mostly poking fun at her politics—Hubbell spots and respects Katie's innate values. He knows that she's a force to be reckoned with, and at a later point in the story tells her that she's beautiful. Though he and Katie seem to be culturally and politically worlds apart, she definitely interests him and he likes her—even though he agrees with her later in the story when she says: "I'm not attractive in the right way. I don't have the right style for you. Do I?"

The Main Story

The DVD describes the story this way:

> "... captivating star-crossed lovers Katie Morosky and Hubbell Gardiner. ...Theirs is a classic love story sparked by the attraction of opposites, played out against the backdrop of American life during times of foreign war, domestic prosperity and McCarthy-era paranoia in Hollywood."

The story begins during the Second World War. Katie has graduated from college and is directing a radio program. After the program she and her producer/writer decide to go to the El Morocco nightclub for a little R&R. There, as if in a dream, she spots Hubbell Gardiner sitting drowsily at the bar dressed in his sailor's uniform (with cap), apparently dozing. She looks at him adoringly and begins to remember their college days.

She remembers her radical campus activities. She remembers that Hubbell was probably the most popular jock at the school and a fabulous writer. He did everything well and with ease. Katie was the practical politico do-gooder who couldn't write a lick, while Hubbell was the genius talent of a writer who surrounded himself with fraternity and sorority rah-rah types.

It wasn't just a one-way attraction, Hubbell was definitely drawn to her. But worlds apart was "the way they were." He knew she was a substantial, interesting person and she knew that he was different than the rest, and beautiful.

And she needed to look at him.

She Arrests His Attention

But first, he arrests hers.

It's the end of their senior year and they have several personal interactions. The first significant one occurs in their English class. Hubbell's story is singled out as the one worthy to be read aloud. The opening sentence slays her. Hubbell writes: "In a way it was like the country he lived in—everything came too easily to him." When they were in the busy library writing these stories, as much as she tried to resist, Katie simply couldn't avert her gaze from fixing on him.

In another scene that takes place in the college café, Hubbell and his vacuous friends are fooling around, poking fun at this or that, and Katie, who is waitressing, gets angry with them.

Hubbell tries to assuage her anger and they have a harmless humorous moment or two. Hubbell tries, but Katie can't join him in his well intentioned attempt to be friendly to her.

Then, in another scene it's a summery evening and Hubbell is having a beer alone at an outdoor café. Here comes Katie walking down the street. He calls her over and they talk. She belatedly congratulates him on his English-class story. He then tells her he actually sold a story, singling her out to share this piece of news because he knows she would understand. And she does. She's thrilled that someone, that Hubbell, sold one. It's the value of writing that she understands, and Hubbell is the writer. Yes, Katie understands it.

Next, we're at the graduation prom. Hubbell walks across the dance floor and cuts in on Katie as she's dancing with Frankie (played by James Woods), her friend and political ally. They do a slow dance but keep at medium arm's length. Hubbell then walks away and out of her life.

The scene returns to Hubbell in his Navy uniform dozing sitting up on a bar stool at the El Morocco night club. He's buzzed, has had too much to drink. Katie spots him, walks over and calls his name. He is startled out of his reverie and looks at her; he immediately knows it's Katie. They wind up at her apartment where he falls dead asleep in her bed. She disrobes and slides in beside him. In his drunken sleep, he rolls over onto her, nuzzles in, and while making love, he falls asleep. A tear streams down Katie's cheek as she quietly proclaims to herself that ". . . he didn't even know it was Katie." In the morning, Hubbell leaves apparently unaware of the togetherness they had shared the night before. He apologizes to her by stating that he might have snored, she responds by telling him she likes snoring.

The Relationship

Within this same time frame Hubbell calls her because he needs a place to stay and they begin their relationship. He has already published a novel. She's read it, as she says, "twice," and they begin to discuss how it could have been deeper. Katie tells him that he stands back rather than getting into the guts of the character and she almost insists that he must write a second novel. This is a telling moment in their relationship because Katie is a doer and always wants the best, while Hubbell doesn't have Katie's drive toward digging for essence.

Their love blossoms into a deep romance. We see them constantly touching one another and kissing and loving to be together. At this point in their loving relationship Hubbell decides to visit his old college friend, J. J. (played by Bradford Dillman) who is at a party on Beekman Place. This is a place that Katie considers elitist and, for two reasons, she resists accompanying him there. The first reason concerns her general disdain for living a capricious elitist capitalist life. The second reason is that this gathering is composed of most of Hubbell's fraternity and sorority college friends—those friends for whom Katie has little respect.

They do attend the party, and Katie has a melt-down—a public impulsive outburst of criticism. Hubbell is embarrassed but he's a stalwart person and forgives her. Nevertheless, their ingrained differences plant the seeds of their eventual separation. Katie can't modulate her distaste for nonsense, and Hubbell can't help but stand back. She admits her outburst was a tantrum and apologizes but Hubbell knows it can't work and leaves. Katie becomes emotionally inconsolable. She calls him sobbing, tells him she needs to see him because he's her best friend, that she can't sleep. Hubbell returns to the nest and they reconcile. He says: "Katie, you expect so much," and she responds by saying: "Oh, but look what I've got" (meaning she's got him and that's a lot). Of course, he gets it that she values him, and she does so for things he has within that he himself, in all likelihood, can't reach.

Hollywood

Now the scene is Hollywood. Hubbell's novel has been sold to be made into a movie and he is adapting the screenplay, with J. J., no less, as the director. When the producer doesn't like what he is doing with the screenplay, Hubbell resists the producer's pleas to make changes. The dilemma Hubbell faces concerns whether he would be willing to forego the entire enterprise rather than capitulate. Katie, of course, would never capitulate, but Hubbell does, and for all intents and purposes, he's humiliated and figuratively speaking, made to crawl.

These are the dramatic days of HUAC (House Un-American Activities Committee). Katie is fighting with all her might to confront the abridgement of liberties represented by the power of this congressional tribunal. Katie and Hubbell are caught in the middle of it all and the tensions of this political whipsaw contribute mightily to the tensions of their relationship.

Hubbell acts out a sexual escapade with Carol Ann (played by Lois Chiles) who is one of Hubbell's old college girlfriends, cut from the same social cloth as he is. She is now the ex wife of J. J. Katie hears about it and even though she's now pregnant, knows that she and Hubbell will no longer ever be together. She knows Hubbell needs to leave but she asks him to stay until the baby is born.

Ban the Bomb

It's now years later and Katie is handing out "Ban the Bomb" leaflets across from the Plaza Hotel in New York City. She spots Hubbell waiting for a cab, he sees her as well. They meet and embrace lovingly. He's with his blonde girlfriend, and Katie herself has now been married for a number of years. In their embrace it's obvious that Katie's obsession with him remains palpable, and it's obvious that he senses what an important person she is. She tells him that their daughter Rachel is beautiful and doing well. Hubbell asks her if her husband is a good father and Katie responds in the absolute affirmative. She invites Hubbell to visit but Hubbell says he can't and Katie says she knows.

They part and what remains is only the way they were.

Katie Morosky on the Couch

This is clearly a story of a *Duet.* It looks a lot like a case of obsessive love. It's pretty clear that Katie had a wild crush on Hubbell when they were in their late teenage years. Later, when they got to know each other as adults, Katie's nerve endings regarding Hubbell kicked up and her sense-memory guided her right back to her deep abiding love for him.

When they first broke up, Katie phoned Hubbell entreating him to help her by returning, even just as a friend so that she could at least sleep. At that point Katie was in a terrible traumatic state very similar to the crushing feeling resulting from unrequited love. It's surely true that if the decision to separate or not was left in Katie's hands, they would have stayed together. But as it was, the decision was always Hubbell's.

It's fairly clear that Hubbell was not obsessed with Katie. Yes, he loved and valued her, but he was not ever completely at home, never completely comfortable with her. Katie knew it because she even referred to not really being his type, or having his "look," and without any hesitation, he concurred.

Furthermore, Hubbell was able to walk away from Rachel, his child with Katie, and never look back. He even agreed to stay with Katie until she gave birth while it was understood that he would leave. This was the case because Hubbell knew that no matter how much Katie loved him, she could never moderate her strident behavior, her absolute stance of rectitude, and her reflexive need to offer strong rejoinders to anyone who disagreed with her position of fair play. Even though she was obsessed with him, her stance of certainty about how life works prevailed even over her obsessive need for him.

This was Katie's problem as well as her strength. The thing she most wanted she couldn't have. What controlled her, even as she wanted Hubbell most, was the way her personality was configured; it compelled her forever more not to be able to satisfy her Hubbell obsession. The dictate of her personality, her sense of justice, was a tyrannical one and it overrode her need to have him. No matter what she wanted and how hard she tried, she couldn't make the bumps in her head fit the holes in his. And so it was not to be.

Katie was able to eventually marry and stay married. But while she does seem happily married, it is obvious that her husband could not ever compensate for her loss of Hubbell, whom she loved rhapsodically. Apparently, this obsessive rhapsodic memory of the way she was, and the way they were, remained as a strong residual need in her psyche and in her feelings.

The Psychology of Obsession

Why do people retain obsessions? The answer is that retaining the obsession with strong residual emotion serves a
phenomenal purpose in one's psychology—in one's psyche.

The purpose the obsession serves in one's psyche is phenomenal because despite the agony of defeat and the suffering of unrequited love defined by the absence of the loved one,
the obsession satisfies something very deep within the person's psyche.

The basic issue is one of retaining the loved one, in camera
as it were, as the better choice—compared to letting it go entirely. This illustrates what Freud meant when he proposed that
in one's psyche, no wish will be denied even if in life—that is,
in reality—the wish is absolutely denied. In Katie's obsessive
state, she has Hubbell; that is, she possesses him at least in
her psyche if not in reality.

But there's more to it and here's the really hidden issue.
Within anyone's love-obsession is hidden repressed anger
toward the loved one. Wherever unrequited love exists there
also exists anger toward the abandoning loved one. But the
anger is not experienced nor realized as existing (by definition, a repressed feeling is not known to the person who
harbors it).

If the anger is relinquished, then the obsession will dis-
solve—in this case, if the obsession dissolves, no more Hubbell. Katie is unconsciously very angry with Hubbell, but she
can't let go of the anger because to do so would mean to relinquish him. Ergo, in her psyche, the anger is kept out of her
awareness. Her obsession means that she would rather continue to suffer with the actual loss of Hubbell into the indefinite

future and possess him in her psyche, rather than end her suffering and lose him totally and forever.

The Nature of Emotional/Psychological Symptoms

As a way to retain the lost object (Hubbell), any person (in this case, Katie) will be quite willing to suffer with an emotional/psychological symptom like an obsession. Freud said this proves that people actually love their symptoms. They love their symptom because having it means possessing in the psyche the special person who was lost in reality but who you can keep safely tucked away forever in your mind.

Katie's obsession with Hubbell seems to be life-long (to this point in her life), and it would be a good guess to say that the obsession will very likely continue for the rest of her life. This is true because the obsession (or whatever might be the symptom) is always the neurotic or perverse gratification of the person's wish. For example, in Katie's case, her wish was for Hubbell to love her and to stay with her. In reality, the wish was thwarted. But in her psyche, in her unconscious mind, of course, the obsession of Hubbell keeps him with her. In this way her wish is gratified—albeit in this neurotic or perverse manner.

Furthermore, it is always the case that the one who in reality thwarts the wish (Hubbell), is the one with whom you feel angry. And that's how symptoms work. She couldn't have him in reality so she keeps him locked away in her heart by way of her unconscious mind and as her unconscious possession.

Were Katie to analyze the obsession this way, there would be a good chance that she would then be able to relinquish the obsession. First, she would have to understand that she's angry and not just in love with him, and second, that to give up the anger would mean to give him up. Presumably, as a result of such analysis, she most likely would finally be able to let him go.

Perhaps the moral of the story is that with some good psychoanalytic work, the way you were is not at all necessarily the way you will always be.

PART 3

TRIOS

Chapter 11

CASABLANCA
(Released, 1942)

From the play, *Everybody Comes To Rick's*
by Murray Burnett and Joan Alison
Written by Julius J. Epstein, Philip G. Epstein,
and Howard Koch
Produced by Hal B. Wallis
Executive Producer: Jack L. Warner
Original Music: Max Steiner
As Time Goes By: Music and Words
by Herman Hupfeld
Directed by Michael Curtiz

Main Cast

Humphrey Bogart	Rick Blaine
Ingrid Bergman	Ilsa Lund
Paul Henreid	Victor Laszlo
Claude Rains	Captain Louis Renault
Conrad Veidt	Major Heinrich Strasser
Sydney Greenstreet	Signor Ferrari
Peter Lorre	Ugarte

S. Z. Sakall	Carl
Madeleine Lebeau	Yvonne
Dooley Wilson	Sam
Joy Page	Annina Brandel
John Qualen	Berger
Leonid Kinskey	Sascha
Curt Bois	Pickpocket

Sample Supporting Cast

Trude Berliner	Baccarat Player at Rick's
Oliver Blake	Waiter at the Blue Parrot
Helmut Dantine	Jan Brandel
Martin Garralaga	Headwaiter at Rick's
George J. Lewis	Haggling Arab Monkey Seller
Jacques Lory	Moor Buying Diamonds
Louis Mercier	Conspirator
Alberto Morin	French Officer Insulting Yvonne
Corinna Mura	Singer with Guitar
Lotte Palfi Andor	Woman Selling Her Diamonds
Richard Ryen	Colonel Heinz — Strasser's Aide
Wolfgang Zilzer	Man with Expired Papers

Introduction

It's Rick's place. It's a nightclub in Casablanca, Morocco. Everybody goes to Rick's and everyone loves Rick (played by Humphrey Bogart), that cynical, swashbuckler, go-it-alone type. Everyone defers to Rick and Rick is the master of his ship, his nightclub. What Rick says, goes. Rick is charismatic and he's got that cool whammy that everyone can feel. Rick is aloof, emotionally remote and indestructible. But then Ilsa shows up—beautiful Ilsa Lund (played by Ingrid Bergman), a woman from his past. And now she needs him. Without missing a beat, Rick almost goes down for the count. But of course, almost, doesn't mean for sure.

It's the Second World War and in order to escape the Nazis, displaced people all over Europe are either wandering, or running, or hiding. In Casablanca, French Morocco, (which is still "free French"—unoccupied by the Nazis) some of these hunted without-a-country wretched souls are awaiting an opportunity to get their hands on an exit visa in order to finally board a flight to Lisbon, Portugal, and then, thank God, to America.

This is the context for the film *Casablanca*. The various themes running through the film are basically subsumed under the general heading of love, and how under certain extreme circumstances such love might be forsaken, renounced, or sacrificed in the service of ideals. Other themes intersect the one of love. These include how people will do anything for survival: compromise one's integrity, double deal, steal, greedily hoard any and all possible advantages, seeking alliances in order to have such advantages, and, even engage in acts of courage and idealism where one's life is in constant and mortal danger.

Putting all of it together makes for an exceedingly full and lavish display of stagecraft: colorful market places crowded with people and overflowing with activity; performers playing instruments and singing; everyone drinking and smoking; excitement in Rick's gambling casino (for fun, as well as gambling in desperation); ubiquitous payoffs and bribes; running from the police; and, of course, competing and searching for those exit visas.

By and large, it's a panoply of action in which one is transported to a magical place—a different place at a different time—where the atmosphere pulsates with life and personal drama all tied together with Rick's place as the center of the action.

The overarching macro-story is, of course, political and ideological where the good guys are outnumbered but who must, at all cost, defeat, outsmart, and even kill the bad guys. Similarly, in the micro-story, innocent love is put to the test, complex love is put to the test, and finally, sacrificial love is put to the test.

And so it was in *Casablanca*.

The Main Story

The DVD describes the story this way:

> "...The time: World War II. The place: Morocco, seething with European refugees desperate for passage to neutral Lisbon. ... Bogart is Rick, a world-weary nightclub owner who claims, 'I stick my neck out for nobody.' Bergman is Ilsa, fleeing the Nazis with her Resistance-hero husband. Only Rick can help the pair escape, but he refuses...until Ilsa reawakens his idealism."

Two German couriers are murdered and their documents taken. These documents are Letters of Transit (exit visas) that may be used as the only way to leave Casablanca for Lisbon—the relay point to the destination desired by all: America. The hunt for these exit visas juices-up everyone's motivation to get them. In the search for the killers, the police chief, Captain Renault (played by Claude Rains) issues the order to "Round up the usual suspects."

Enter Sam (played by Dooley Wilson) who is the one constant in Rick's entourage. He's sitting at his piano playing, *It Had To Be You,* a tune with a definite foreshadowing. The tune symbolizes that there is only one love in Rick's life. But where is she, and who is she, who it had to be? While we're waiting for her to appear in Casablanca, everyone else is trying to leave Casablanca—to escape.

The person who has the Letters of Transit, those exit visas, is Ugarte (played by Peter Lorre). It's understood that Ugarte probably killed the Germans and thereby acquired the exit visas. Ugarte begs Rick to take the Letters of Transit for safe keeping because he knows he may be apprehended by the police. Rick takes them and surreptitiously slips them under the lid at the top of the upright piano; he does this in the throes of nightclub life when the lights are down low and entertainment is at its height. Rick is cool, so no one sees it.

In the midst of all of it, this same Rick Blaine, in his white tuxedo evening jacket, is busy solving all sorts of problems that occur in such a setting. He carries out these tasks with great aplomb, and at the same time reveals a distinctly cynical attitude about life. He's a hip-talking, world-weary, experienced cynic—but despite his protestations to the contrary, he's really got a heart of gold. His cynicism shows however, while his heart of gold is under lock and key. In fact he says, and later repeats: "I stick my neck out for nobody."

Rick's friendship with Captain Renault is obvious. He hands Renault payoffs and Renault accepts them without a trace of shame. The implicit understanding is that Rick will not to be bothered by the police, and his nightclub will remain problem-free and always open for business. Rick does this by permitting Renault to win at roulette, a fact which tells us that the roulette table is fixed.

Enter Ilsa

Here she comes (everyone comes to Rick's). After seeing Ilsa, Rick sits alone in a drunken stupor in his darkened office directly above the main floor of his nightclub, cursing his fate to be without her.

She's with her husband, Victor Laszlo (played by Paul Henreid), the leader of the French anti-Nazi resistance. The authorities of Casablanca, namely Captain Renault and Major Strasser (the Nazi in charge, played by Conrad Veidt), agree that Laszlo is not to leave Casablanca. No exit visa for Laszlo! Laszlo had escaped from a Nazi concentration camp where he had been brutalized. Anti-Nazi fighters rally around him, a high-value capture because of his reputation as a miracle-man and a protest leader.

Strasser questions Rick, and in the process, implies that America will fall, to which Rick sardonically answers that there are "certain sections of New York that I wouldn't advise you to invade."

Laszlo and Ilsa walk into Rick's. She spots Sam, a person from her past when she and Rick had a magnificent, rhapsodic love affair in Paris. Later in the story Ilsa confesses to Rick that at the time they had their love affair, she had been told that Laszlo was dead. She got the news that he was alive just as she and Rick were about to leave Paris because the Germans were storming the city. Once she knew that Laszlo was alive, she couldn't leave with Rick. She left Rick waiting for her at the train station with a goodbye note delivered by Sam.

While in Rick's, Laszlo meets with other individuals who are aligned with him in spirit as well as in action, and who with pride, identify themselves as French resistance fighters. At the same time, Ilsa talks to Sam. "Where's Rick, Sam," she asks? Sam tries to stall her but she asks him to "Play it Sam." Sam knows the song she wants to hear and tries not to, but Ilsa says, "Play *As Time Goes By*." Sam begins playing and singing it. Upon hearing it, Rick quickly walks over to Sam and starts to scold him by telling him, "I told you never to play. . . ." Sam motions toward Ilsa. Rick sees her and almost craters. But he hangs on. They talk and Rick, striking out in anger, reminds her that when they were in Paris, the Germans wore grey while she wore blue. Rick acknowledges Laszlo's importance, but still doesn't know why she disappeared rather than catching the train with him, except that now he knows she's with Laszlo.

It is after that when Rick, sitting in his office at night in a drunken stupor, says those 'destiny' words out loud to himself: "Of all the gin joints of all the towns in the world, she walks into mine."

Paris

Rick remembers Paris. We see them in Paris, very much in love. Rick is a happy man without a trace of cynicism or anger. We follow their comings and goings, and how each is perplexed about not knowing very much about the other. Ilsa says, "No questions." Rick pours her some champagne and says, "Here's looking at you kid." Ilsa says, "There was a man in my life. He's dead." At the same time, the Germans announce their impending arrival and Rick and Ilsa know that the blacklist the Germans have will put them in grave danger. "With the whole world crumbling, we pick this time to fall in love," Rick says.

"I'll meet you at the station," Ilsa says. She has discovered that Laszlo is alive and so she turns down Rick's offer to pick her up and go to the station together. Ilsa knows, but Rick doesn't, that there will be no meeting at the station. Rick proposes marriage and Ilsa starts to cry. She says, "I love you so much, and I hate this war so much." She implies, without saying it, that this is their last time together.

Sam delivers Ilsa's note at the station:

> "Richard, I cannot go with you or ever see you
> again. You must not ask why. Just believe me
> that I love you. Go my darling, and God bless
> you. Ilsa."

Rick and Sam get on the train and the train pulls out of Paris.

Rick's Nightclub

It's very late at night. The club is closed and Ilsa enters Rick's office. She begins to tell Rick about her relationship with Laszlo. Apparently at first Laszlo was like a father to her and she worshipped him. Rick doesn't want to hear it. Compared to how Rick was in love with Ilsa in Paris, how he adored her, and how he was such a nice optimistic guy, he is now dejected and bitter. He has turned into a man filled with pessimism, cynicism, and his sense of the corrupt disappointing world. It's obvious that his wounded heart has never healed.

A day or two later they spot one another in the market place and Ilsa finally tells Rick that Laszlo is her husband. She adds that he was her husband even when Rick and she had their love affair in Paris, although at that time she thought Laszlo had been killed. Now, the plot is building to the point where Ilsa is going to need to make a decision: Laszlo or Rick.

Laszlo tells Ilsa that he loves her very much. He goes to Rick and asks for help getting the exit visas but Rick won't help and tells him to ask Ilsa why. Laszlo reminds Rick that his freedom is important to thousands of people. But, it's a no-go with Rick. Laszlo knows that in the past Rick had smuggled arms to the rebels fighting for freedom in Ethiopia, and that he also fought against the fascists in Spain. Nevertheless, as far as Rick is concerned, all of that now falls on deaf ears.

Interestingly, Rick has made arrangements to sell his night-club to Signor Ferrari (played by Sydney Greenstreet), owner of the *Blue Parrot*, another nightclub. As part of the deal, he sees to it that Sam will keep his job with a nice pay raise, and that Rick's other employees will keep their jobs as well. The question is: What in the world is going on? Apparently, Rick is making plans to leave Casablanca.

For the second time Laszlo tells Ilsa that he loves her very much, and for the second time she does not reply in kind. Ilsa again goes to see Rick. She tells him she needs those exit visas, and she points a pistol at him. Rick calmly says: "Go ahead, shoot, you'll be doing me a favor." Ilsa then creates the beginning of the end of the story by confessing her love to him: "If you knew how much I loved you, how much I still love you." She tells Rick how she heard about Laszlo's survival from the concentration camp the very day they were going to leave Paris. And now she states, in no uncertain terms the very thing that Rick has been dreaming about: "I'll never have the strength to leave you again. I can't fight it anymore. You have to speak for both of us."

Because Laszlo feels that Rick won't supply him with the Letters of Transit, he takes a difficult step and implores Rick to take Ilsa out of Casablanca on the next plane so that at least Ilsa would eventually be safe.

In a seemingly illogical tactic, and in a counterintuitive moment, Rick then cooks up a plan that tricks Captain Renault into releasing Laszlo from the detention into which he had been placed. The question is why free Laszlo when Rick's gotten what he's most wanted in the world?

Rick pulls a gun on Renault and tells him to call the airport. Instead, Renault tricks Rick by calling Strasser and talking to him about the airport as though he was talking to some airport controller. Rick, Ilsa, and Renault are at the airport when Strasser arrives. Rick shoots and kills Strasser. Renault, leaps to Rick's side and tells the arriving police that Strasser has been killed and that they should: "Round up the usual suspects."

Rick, Ilsa, Renault, and Laszlo are all standing and waiting for the plane that is about to land. Suddenly, Rick makes it clear that he will remain, and Ilsa will be leaving with Laszlo. Ilsa remembers that she had told him that he had to make decisions for both of them. Rick explains that if she remained with him and abandoned Laszlo, eventually she would regret it, and as a result, the relationship between Rick and Ilsa would no longer work. So the best possible result—no matter the pain—is for her to stay with Laszlo.

("Here's looking at you, kid.")

Rick has taken the high ground. Ilsa is terribly unhappy —even crushed, because although she does have great feeling and love for Laszlo, her love for Rick is of the rapturous, libidinous kind, and that's different than the apparent platonic love she has for Victor.

Ilsa and Laszlo walk to the plane and it takes off, flying Ilsa away from Casablanca and forever out of Rick's life. Rick and Renault decide to get out of Casablanca through other means, and at the end this is a redeeming moment for them both.

As Rick and Renault walk toward the evening darkness, Rick ends the movie by saying: "Louie, I think this is the start of a beautiful friendship."

Ilsa Lund On The Couch

Ilsa is in a terrible fix. She has the impossible dilemma. She loves two men and each loves her, and each wants to spend his life with her. One is her husband and one is her lover. It is this perfect triangle that invites such a story to be included in the category identified in this book, as *Trios*. One love is an idealistic love based on high principles of sacrifice and belief in the goodness of man, while the other is a libidinous, luscious love full of romance and all ecstatic wishes realized. At one time Ilsa gave up the latter (Rick), for the former (Victor) but now she feels she can't do that again. She wants the romance. Yes, she wants Rick, but she's very confused and overwhelmed, and leaves it all in Rick's hands to know what to do. And Rick definitely knows what to do. He tells her she must go with her husband.

The psychoanalytic question is: Why?

The answer can be found in Ilsa's history. Originally she was taken over by Victor Laszlo (idealized him) because he was known for his courageous idealistic exploits. At the time she was just a young girl. She simply adored him, and eventually adoration and love fused. Further in the relationship she grew to love Victor in a more adult way. He introduced her to very important and productive work in the service of humanity and civility and to the value of freedom. Ilsa became educated within the parameters of a cause and Victor Laszlo was the central image of that cause. When it was reported to her that he had been killed, she had been terribly traumatized. Then she met Rick in Paris, and he pulled her out of her misery. She immersed herself in him in such a way that their love affair became one for the ages.

With this little preamble in mind, a little psychoanalytic insight is useful. You see, the relationship Victor and Ilsa first had was almost as father to daughter. In that sense it had a distinctly platonic cast to it even though because of their conjugal relationship we know that there was certainly a sexual component to their relationship. Usually when a relationship starts where a rescue of sorts is taking place, one partner will be the rescuer while the other is the rescued. In a father/daughter relationship the father is the rescuer while the daughter is the rescued. Parent rescues child. Or, another way of putting it is to say that the parent figure is the dominant one just as is the rescuer, and the child figure is the recessive or submissive one, just as is the rescued.

However, what usually happens in rescuer/rescued situations is that eventually the dominant one becomes the one

who needs the help and the submissive one becomes dominant. This is seen time and again in typical more dominant to
less dominant relationships. In other words, the relationship,
flip-flops. This is precisely what happened to Ilsa and Victor.
Eventually, Ilsa became the parent helping Victor, who in turn,
and in an analogous way, became the child. Victor even says
that he needs her help. Therefore, what started out between
Victor and Ilsa as a relationship with a father/daughter cast
to it, gradually evolved into a relationship with a mother/son
cast.

And Now, This is It

And now we arrive at the linchpin to the entire issue regarding why Rick sends Ilsa on her way. The DVD indicates that he
did it because she awakened his idealism. However, a more
personal, emotional truth may be that the choice that Rick understood, or at least intuited, was that a normal mother can
never abandon her child in favor of her lover. Never! And if
she did, she would live to regret it. It is wired into her DNA that
her child must, at all cost, be protected and never abandoned.
Therefore Ilsa must leave Casablanca with Victor because in
a way she is the mother and Victor is the child. Rick even told
Ilsa that if she remained with him she would live to regret it. A
person like Victor, who is so absolute in an ideal or cause, is in
some way, and in a non-pejorative sense, innocent and pure,
like a child.

So, Ilsa doesn't really have a choice; she absolutely cannot
abandon Victor no matter how much she pleads for Rick to
make the choice for her.

P.S.:

Now for the bad news. It's about Sam.

Parenthetically, despite the ideology of good is good and bad is bad, Sam is treated in the film with typical stereotyped pejorative language, with disparaging attitudes which in those days were directed to people referred to as "colored." Since the early 1940's, the evolution of "colored" has been denoted sequentially as colored, Negro, black, and African-American. We know that this evolution of reference is really an evolving search for solid identity.

The point is that Rick and Sam are friends, but Rick acts like a boss. Sam, at one point, actually refers to Rick as Mr. Richards. At another point in the story Rick gets angry at Sam because he is playing *As Time Goes By* on the piano. Still, Sam never shows any sign of the unfairness of it all. At another point, Ilsa refers to Sam as the "boy" over there at the piano.

Perhaps the most egregious behavior toward Sam is that while sometimes Rick is quite buddy-buddy with Sam, he can become hostile at the drop of a hat. All the while Sam is at Rick's side behaving almost as his slave/friend—no less, his willing slave/friend.

It becomes necessary to point this out because Bogart himself had always been egalitarian and yet, for whatever reason, Sam's role was not challenged by anyone associated with this film—a film that was completely anti-facist/anti-Nazi, as well as being implicitly all American in terms of the American ideal of equality. The argument that in those days that's how black people were treated is not valid because the setting of the story was not set in Mississippi in 1942. Rather, we're talking about Casablanca, in North Africa.

In addition, the answer that the film was a period piece where African-Americans were treated that way, again, doesn't really wash here because of Bogart's social consciousness. Also, in the film, Bergman plays the wife of the leader of the anti-Nazis. With Ingrid Bergman also playing a socially conscious individual who is risking her life for her ideals, all of it together would be a perfect arena to lobby for Sam to be an equal even though he's in Rick's employ.

The truth in the movie is that on one hand, there is a sharp distinction made between each of the employees who work at Rick's, and on the other hand, there is Rick himself as the boss. He's the boss and there's no doubt about it. And despite Rick's tough demeanor, it's obvious that all his employees love him, as does Sam, because they really know about his heart of gold. However, in Sam's case, the disparaging stereotyped language as well as the attitude displayed toward him is an even sharper distinction between him and Rick than is any other distinction between Rick and any other employee (with the exception of his ex-girlfriend, Yvonne [played by Madeleine Lebeau], who Rick treats poorly).

The Sam issue is a terrible nasty flaw in the film and shouldn't be overlooked. Therefore, if we put Hollywood itself on the couch we would need to notice that in Hollywood, writers, producers, casting directors, and directors usually shoot for images that offer instant recognition. And so unfortunately, it seems that stereotyping in Hollywood becomes endemic.

But there's more.

The question becomes: Who gets what they want and who doesn't? Let's start with Rick. Rick is essentially involved in a geometry of dramas. On the one hand a scenario exists in the triangle composed of him, Ilsa, and Victor Laszlo, out of which arises a dyad in which Victor is the victor—he walks away with the prize, Ilsa. A second triangle involves Rick, Sam, and Signor Ferrari (owner of the *Blue Parrot*), out of which arises another dyad in which Ferrari is now the owner of Rick's nightclub as well as owner of the *Blue Parrot*. A third triangle involves the deal in which Sam is 'adopted' by Ferrari in the arrangement that Rick and Ferrari make in the transfer of *Rick's* to Ferrari. Even though Rick gets assurances from Ferrari that Sam and the other employees will continue to be employed at *Rick's*, essentially, Sam is sold out, or just plainly sold!

But there's still more.

Now, the question is: Who are the winners and who are the losers? The answer is of course, that there are several losers, beginning with Rick. He loses his cabaret. Ilsa loses Rick, but in the end, she is the mother who didn't abandon her child. And now, Sam loses Rick. The trade off for Rick in losing Sam is the acquisition of Renault. Not a good trade, but actually signaling a new phase in Rick's life and not merely a continuation of the past. However, in losing Sam, Rick becomes the abandoning parent (Sam had been Rick's sidekick), and this is what makes Rick truly a tragic figure. He becomes what he prevented Ilsa from becoming.

Thus, the tragic trade-off at the end of this entirely involving story seems to be that Rick must give up everything (Ilsa, his cabaret, and Sam), he loses in all of the triangles, in order to presumably finally find himself.

In the end, the profound moral of the story might be that in finding yourself things go wrong, and in addition, you must lose.

Is that possible?

Chapter 12

THE GRADUATE
(Released, 1967)

From the novel, *The Graduate,* by Charles Webb
Screenplay by Calder Willingham / Buck Henry
Produced by Lawrence Turman
Executive Producer: Joseph E. Levine
Original Music by Paul Simon / Dave Grusin
Mrs. Robinson by Paul Simon
Sung by Paul Simon & Art Garfunkel
Directed by Mike Nichols

Main Cast

Anne Bancroft	Mrs. Robinson
Dustin Hoffman	Ben Braddock
Katharine Ross	Elaine Robinson
William Daniels	Mr. Braddock
Murray Hamilton	Mr. Robinson
Elizabeth Wilson	Mrs. Braddock

Supporting Sample Cast

Buck Henry	Room Clerk
Richard Dreyfuss	Boarding House Resident

Brian Avery	Carl Smith
Walter Brooke	Mr. McGuire
Norman Fell	Mr. McCleery
Alice Ghostley	Mrs. Singleman
Marion Lorne	Miss DeWittee

Introduction

Well, hello Mrs. Robinson. How can one person cause so much trouble? I know you don't really care that you've affected everyone's life around you. The fact is that your little escapade with Benjamin detonated like an atom bomb and radiated everyone you knew—including you.

You took a confused kid, barely out of college and turned him inside out. You made him do it. He was aimlessly drifting, and you gave him first a preoccupation and then an occupation. Seduction was your game; a chance for him to ruminate you, to be preoccupied with you, and then you also gave him an occupation—being busy with your body. You essentially said to him: 'Benjamin, even though I'm your mother's age, I'm going to draw you down into the eddy, into my vortex, where I can lose myself by taking you there. I will make you want to do what I want you to do. And because you yourself are experiencing it, you actually think this story is about you. Well, my little boy, it's not at all about you. It's about me!'

"You see, Benjamin, I'm the spoiler; I'm Mrs. Robinson."

The Graduate is a story about an older woman, Mrs. Robinson (played by Anne Bancroft) and a younger man, Benjamin Braddock (played by Dustin Hoffman). The young man's mother, Mrs. Braddock (played by Elizabeth Wilson) is Mrs. Robinson's friend, and Mr. Braddock, the young man's father (played by William Daniels) is the business partner of Mrs. Robinson's husband, (played by Murray Hamilton). Thus, there are two main couples: the Braddocks and the Robinsons. Benjamin is the Braddocks' son, and Elaine Robinson (played by Katharine Ross) is the Robinsons' daughter.

The Main Story

The DVD describes the story as:

> "Shy Benjamin Braddock returns home from college with an uncertain future. Then the wife of his father's business partner, the sexy Mrs. Robinson seduces him, and the affair only deepens his confusion. That is, until he meets the girl of his dreams. But there's one problem: She's Mrs. Robinson's daughter!"

The opening scene begins with Benjamin Braddock coming home from college. He's graduated. As the plane is arriving at the airport, the pilot announces that the plane is now in a descent into Los Angeles. Of course the operative term in the pilot's declaration is "descending" as in "descent." And a descent it is because Benjamin is at a loss to know what to do with his life. He is, as he puts it, "worried about the future."

As we meet Benjamin, in the background we hear Paul Simon and Art Garfunkel singing *The Sounds of Silence*: "Hello darkness my old friend," along with "people talking without speaking" and "listening without hearing." This is the problem that Benjamin faces. No one's talking to him without the use of ubiquitous and trite clichés, and perhaps worse, no one's listening to him. Although his parents and his parents' friends are throwing all sorts of advice his way concerning his future, no one is really speaking his language. Mr. McGuire (played by Walter Brooke) a family friend, has the answer. McGuire tells Benjamin that he wants to speak to him about something very important concerning his future. Dramatically, McGuire asks Benjamin if he is listening to him. Of course, Benjamin answers in the affirmative and Mr. McGuire lays it on him. Referring to Benjamin's future, he tells Benjamin that he's only going to say one word—pausing and building up dramatic tension making it seem as though this will be the magic word that can ensure Benjamin's future.

"Plastics!"

Quickly, Benjamin retreats to his upstairs bedroom. On his way up, he passes a painting of a clown hanging on the wall. He takes a quick look at the clown that appears to be staring back at him. It's only a brief glance but it's symbolic, and not at all lost on us.

According to Benjamin, "plastics" is what defines his parents and their friends. It's pretty obvious that Benjamin will make sure that "plastics" will never be about him!

Here She Comes

And then it happens. All of the Braddock's friends are at the Braddock house celebrating Benjamin's graduation and homecoming. In the middle of the party Mrs. Robinson asks Benjamin to drive her home. Benjamin really doesn't want to, but he can't refuse her, as she is a close friend of the family and speaks with assumed authority. She tells him that Mr. Robinson will not be home, and that she's apprehensive about entering a dark house alone. She adds that he will need to escort her into the house and stay awhile because she doesn't like to be alone.

At each of Mrs. Robinson's invitations, Benjamin directly expresses reluctance. Yet, in a situation such as this where Mrs. Robinson is the mature woman, and Benjamin only an inexperienced confused young man, her influence is equivalent to that of, let us say, a dominatrix.

It becomes clear immediately that Mrs. Robinson instinctively knows how to control Benjamin. We begin to see Mrs. Robinson's careful, deliberate, and unrelenting momentum as she surrounds him, not permitting him to breathe or think, making him a slave to her wishes.

Once inside, Mrs. Robinson begins to discuss her personal life. Sitting on the stool at her bar with her short skirt pulled up above her knees, she crosses her legs provocatively so Benjamin, very uncomfortable at being placed in this situation, directly tells her that she's opening up her personal life to him and asks if she's trying to seduce him. Of course, the correspondence between how her legs are positioned and how she's similarly opening up her personal life is no accident.

Mrs. Robinson knows exactly what she's doing.

She asks Benjamin to accompany her up to Elaine's bedroom to see Elaine's portrait. There, turning her back to him, she asks Benjamin to unzip her dress. With the grace of a gazelle, Mrs. Robinson is able to confront Benjamin in her bra and panties. She's got him in a claustrophobic panic. At the same time, and not a moment too soon, Mr. Robinson's car is heard coming into the driveway. Benjamin bolts downstairs to the living room as Mr. Robinson enters the house.

Mr. Robinson is happy to see Benjamin. They talk, and Mr. Robinson then encourages Benjamin to take some time off and sow some wild oats, to have some "flings." Mr. Robinson comes across as an obvious sap. Benjamin's parents also seem out of touch with his needs. None of them know how to guide him, or offer him structure, or reflect his feelings, or suggest what he might want, and not what they might want.

None of them can do that, with the exception of Mrs. Robinson. She knows how to suggest a structure to Benjamin that will organize all of his evenings—in bed with her. With Mrs. Robinson at the helm, there are no elective courses. There is only one course, and it is required—to do as she wishes. And she tells Benjamin what she wishes—to call her whenever he should want to.

The Hotel

We see Benjamin doing pretty much nothing productive. He lays around his house doing nothing, or floating in his pool doing nothing. Benjamin finally calls Mrs. Robinson and invites her to the Taft Hotel. She meets him there, and a hilarious and somewhat sad and anxious series of events unfolds and Benjamin's lack of experience becomes obvious—in ordering drinks at the bar, in simply finding a place for himself in the lobby of the hotel, and in checking in for a room. Finally, he and Mrs. Robinson find themselves in a room together.

Mrs. Robinson is task-oriented. She begins stripping but Benjamin tries to delay the inevitable. No such luck, because Mrs. Robinson knows which button to press and without hesitation she presses it. When she suggests that Benjamin might feel "inadequate," that does it. The deal is done and Benjamin hops to it. The serial assignations begin and they meet each night at the hotel and go to it—all the while Benjamin continues to address her as "Mrs. Robinson." She, of course, couldn't care less about what Benjamin calls her. All she wants is to undress and continue to act-out this strange drama of a sexy, attractive mature woman fucking her brains out night after night with a boy-toy who she really couldn't care less about. To drive that point home, she never ever engages him in simple conversation.

Even Benjamin, this innocent young man, finally suggests that it would be a good idea to talk. But she resists this suggestion and is blunt in her response: "What should we talk about?" Translation: "There is nothing to talk about!"

Benjamin's parents are curious and question him about where he goes each night but he doesn't answer them. Along with Mr. Robinson, Benjamin's parents begin pressuring him to date the Robinsons' daughter, Elaine. Mrs. Robinson knows about the campaign and commands Benjamin never to date Elaine. Benjamin agrees, and that's that—or at least, it seems to be.

Even though Benjamin resists parental pressures to date Elaine, circumstances force him to make the date. Mrs. Robinson has a fit over it and in no uncertain terms tells Benjamin he is not to go through with it. Benjamin says he really doesn't have any feeling for Elaine but to mollify his parents as well as Mr. Robinson, he will do it and get it over with.

Elaine

As fate would have it, Elaine is pretty, very nice and understanding, and she likes Benjamin. But Benjamin can't see the forest for the trees and is blinded by his own problems as well as by Mrs. Robinson's command. On their first date, Benjamin humiliates Elaine by taking her to a strip club in a down-and-out neighborhood. Elaine bolts. Benjamin realizes that he's behaved entirely out of character is horrified at what he's done. He quickly catches up to her and profusely apologizes. His honesty and sincerity are not to be denied. Elaine gradually calms down and forgives him.

Then the inevitable happens; they become fast friends and can talk about anything—well, almost anything. We now have a profound dilemma, one of stratospheric proportions. How in the world is Benjamin going to tell Elaine that he's screwing her mother and then expect this flowering romance of theirs to evolve? He can't.

We know that this deep secret is going to be revealed, and when it is, look out! And so it happens that Mrs. Robinson, Benjamin, and Elaine are together when Elaine asks Benjamin whether he's having an affair with an older woman. Her question is prompted by Benjamin's erratic behavior, he seems to be hiding something. After Elaine asks that question both Benjamin and Mrs. Robinson become visibly caught in the headlights. In a split second pause, Elaine sees them both, and realizes who the older woman is.

Well, that's it for Benjamin, and that's it for Mrs. Robinson's relationship with her daughter. Now Benjamin is at his lowest. He's in agony about losing Elaine who has returned to college. At this point the story is in its final act, with Benjamin beginning to climb the mountain from ground zero in order to finally be in the ascendancy and recapture his promising relationship with Elaine. He announces to his parents that he's going to marry her.

Benjamin is off to Elaine's college where at first he secretly watches her from afar. He's a harmless voyeur. Finally, he makes himself visible to her but she resists his overtures and they make no progress towards togetherness. Next, Mr. Robinson shows up. Where he had once behaved as a mentor to Benjamin, he is now furious because he knows about Benjamin's dalliance with his wife. He confronts Benjamin, but it becomes clear why Mrs. Robinson might have felt the need to escape his rather unformed masculinity. He's afraid of contact —afraid of getting hurt. He's even afraid that Benjamin might attack him. So in the absence of any physical confrontation, he just spouts off and leaves.

Elaine then disappears and the next thing we see is that she's marrying one of her suitors. Marriage plans are pulled quickly together by her parents, obviously in order to seal a membrane around Elaine specifically designed to keep Benjamin out. But Benjamin puts the puzzle pieces together and discovers the location of the wedding ceremony. He frantically gets to the church just as the marriage vows are being pronounced, and through a large closed glass partition he begins shouting "Elaine, Elaine, Elaine."

Elaine turns to see Benjamin in his state of disarray and chaotic panic, but also senses his laser sharp focus. She is startled and suddenly awakened by Benjamin's hypnotic presence, his pleading insistence that she abort the ceremony, and take this last train out with him. She does it!

Elaine dramatically flees the ceremony. As the movie ends, they run together to catch a bus, leaving their otherwise impossible lives behind. They've made it.

Whether it's a matter of justice or punishment, Mrs. Robinson remains alone without her friends, without her husband, without her daughter, and of course, without Benjamin.

Mrs. Robinson on the Couch

Psychologically, it's Mrs. Robinson's movie because she's the pivotal character around whom five triangular relationships exist. An oedipal bouquet is the ubiquitous aroma in all five. Obviously, it places the story squarely in the category of *Trios*.

The issue is oedipal because a somewhat incestuous older woman/younger man liaison sets it all off. However, the precursor to it all concerns the relationship between the two couples who are friends with each other. The couples are Mr. and Mrs. Braddock, the parents of Benjamin, and Mr. and Mrs. Robinson, the parents of Elaine.

Mrs. Robinson Contaminates Everyone Within Her Geometry of Triangles

Triangle #1. Mrs. Robinson, Benjamin, and Benjamin's mother, Mrs. Braddock.

In Triangle #1, when Mrs. Robinson "takes" Benjamin, she is implicating herself in a possession competition with Mrs. Braddock, Benjamin's mother. In this first category of triangulation, Mrs. Robinson triumphs over Mrs. Braddock. She "takes" Mrs. Braddock's son at will.

Triangle #2. Mrs. Robinson, Benjamin, and Mr. Robinson.

In Triangle #2, Mrs. Robinson defeats her own husband, implicitly humiliating him by rendering him impotent in the face of her preference for a boy over him. When Mrs. Robinson "takes" Benjamin, she is "dissing" or defeating Mr. Robinson.

Triangle #3. Mrs. Robinson, Benjamin, and Benjamin's father, Mr. Braddock.

In Triangle #3, Mrs. Robinson defeats Mr. Braddock because she pays him no mind as a man, while preferring his son. When Mrs. Robinson "takes" Benjamin, she reduces Mr. Braddock to a non-person.

Triangle #4. Mrs. Robinson, Benjamin, and Benjamin's parents as a couple.

In Triangle #4, when Mrs. Robinson "takes" Benjamin, she is lording it over both Mr. and Mrs. Braddock as a parental couple. Despite her own role as a parent, she nevertheless endows herself as having access to powers that also make her a distinct sexual being. This consigns Mr. and Mrs. Braddock to the history bin—both are no longer relevant nor even aware enough to know what's happening to their only adult child.

Triangle # 5. Mrs. Robinson, Benjamin, and Mrs. Robinson's daughter, Elaine.

In Triangle #5, Mrs. Robinson partials her own daughter out of the sexual competition by rigging the election. When Mrs. Robinson "takes" Benjamin, she is dueling with her own daughter for the alpha female position and as a foregone conclusion, she wins.

It is true that Benjamin is a key player. However, it was not Benjamin who initiated and then ignited this multifaceted drama of triangulation. In fact, Benjamin was horrified at Mrs. Robinson's initial advances. His innocence, as well as his natural instinct that forbade incest (Mrs. Robinson was a mother equivalent), motivated him do everything he could to resist her. Of course the question is: How is a young man of Benjamin's age (with those hormones coursing through his body) going to resist a predatory and determined Mrs. Robinson who insists on showing him her body and then ordering him to take it?

Without a doubt, Mrs. Robinson is at the controls in each of the triangles.

As a significant part of her fantasy life, Mrs. Robinson's psychological motive in these triangular relationships is to wield power over each of them. It is how she can feel liberated from the din of her life. In addition, it's her seductive acting-out behavior that reflects her contempt and disdain for her life and everyone in it (most especially and probably her husband). So, the question becomes how is she going to express this contempt? And the answer she presents is to act-out a resounding "Fuck You" to everyone involved—by doing *it*. By doing *what*? The answer is by seducing, then possessing, and then using Benjamin as the vehicle that ultimately expresses her implosive / explosive life.

Benjamin of course is an overtly and apparently confused and drifting individual, but Mrs. Robinson is the one who is actually and profoundly covertly confused. She has essentially removed herself from her friends, the Braddocks, and with malice aforethought, contaminated their son. At some point Benjamin will need to understand all the implications of their affair or at least how it relates to his mother and father.

It Might Be A Happy Ending

Benjamin was simply Mrs. Robinson's sacrificial tool. Despite the fact that he wanted to talk and not just jump into bed, she reluctantly humored that civilized impulse of his, then dismissed it, and finally told him what his job was — his only job.

As long as Mrs. Robinson could have her way with him, she could realize her basic wish — to be removed from her life with these aging people who are happy with clichés and trite nonsense. That was what she acted out. In reality however, one of her very important problems was that her affair with Benjamin could never ever be kept secret.

In the final analysis, Mrs. Robinson gave up on all of her friends, and in the end, Elaine, because of her mother's oedipal situation, gave up on her mother. Now, counting the cast of characters, Mrs. Robinson lost all of her friends, she lost Benjamin, is in the process of losing her husband, and most importantly, lost her daughter.

The moral of the story is expressed between those people who will usually opt for the impossible, and who forget that in life it's probably good to eschew the complicated and keep things as simple as possible. It may be that the objective in life is to simplify!

With that in mind, we can see that Mrs. Robinson, is now alone.

Perhaps the issue most hidden is the underlying commonality that enables the story to be pieced together in the first place. It's really a story of the interaction between two characters who are the most unsettled and dissatisfied with their lives. These are the ones who are the most vulnerable: Benjamin who is confused and thereby susceptible to any irrepressible force and, Mrs. Robinson, who is present as the irrepressible force — incarnate, in the flesh!

Chapter 13

THE GHOST AND MRS. MUIR
(Released, 1947)

From the novel, *The Ghost and Mrs. Muir*, by R.A. Dick
Screenplay by Philip Dunne
Produced by Fred Kohlmar
Original Music by Bernard Herrmann
Directed by Joseph L. Mankiewicz

Main Cast

Gene Tierney	Lucy Muir
Rex Harrison	Capt. Daniel Gregg
George Sanders	Miles Fairley
Edna Best	Martha Huggins
Vanessa Brown	Anna Muir as an Adult
Anna Lee	Mrs. Miles Fairley
Robert Coote	Mr. Coombe
Natalie Wood	Anna Muir as a Child
Isobel Elsom	Angelica, Mother-in-law
Victoria Horne	Eva, Sister-in-law
Whitford Kane	Sproule, London Publisher

Sample Supporting Cast

Buster Slaven	Enquiries at Sproule's
William Stelling	Bill, Anna's Fiancee
David Thursby	Mr. Scroggins
Heather Wilde	Fairley Maid

Introduction

You're beautiful, a widow for a year, and now living with your late husband's family. You are trying to escape it all and live by the ocean, more or less alone, when you fall in love with a dashing seafaring ghost that's inhabiting the house at the ocean. To top it off, you can talk to him. Do you fall in love? And if so, what does it mean that you fall in love with a ghost? Can you be rescued from this impossible fate of loving a ghost, and what if, per chance, this ghost also deeply loves you?

The Ghost and Mrs. Muir is a love story with a bittersweet underpinning. It's a wishful fantasy but it's also mournful. It's a story about pain that can only be assuaged in the distant future while in the present, this pain, longing, and loneliness, is powdered over with sincerity, and beauty, and a lovely place to live overlooking the ocean—in a cottage—alone—almost alone, but most importantly, away from the din.

It's a story about the tension of living one's life alone and awaiting the end. In the process of awaiting this end, one can be enchanted with the colors and forms of life, as well as with appreciations of all sorts. Yet, in another way, it's a story about going through the motions of living in the real world, but in fact, actually living 'behind-the-line' in dreams and fantasies and wishes and melancholy—all of it embraced in a misty, ghostly, withdrawal.

In her solitude, Lucy Muir (played by Gene Tierney) can romanticize her beautiful surroundings and be enthralled with how this living arrangement offers her serenity and peace of mind. She is quite okay with illusion. Rather than struggling with the tension-producing events of the real world (that are always impinging and challenging everyone), she has withdrawn to a lovely seaside cottage to spend the rest of her days taking walks along the ocean.

To Choose

Is one persuaded more by reality and the struggle required to work out the problems and tensions created by the real world, or is one more persuaded by an internal signal—one in your gut, in your heart, in your groin, in your psyche? The internal signal—impulses and needs—want to be expressed and satisfied; they want to be fully realized. The quest for such delicious gratification is fueled by a highly seductive urge within the person who is nursing them and cherishing them. This is the stuff of dreams, of the person's sense of true self—of those impulses and needs that exist within and that know no external rules and regulations.

Some people feel that the struggle between being in the real world versus withdrawing from it, is too big—too difficult to manage. For them, withdrawal into fantasy and into some ideal tension-free condition is preferable to living in the real world. In extreme withdrawal we get conditions of mental and emotional instability. However, it is possible to create a bubble in which one can simply dream, and wish, and hope for peace of mind.

The possibility exists that rather than a complete mental and emotional withdrawal, one can create conditions to minimize contact with the outside world and yet maintain some residual connections and relationships.

Enter, Lucy Muir.

The Main Story

The DVD describes the story this way:

> "Recent widow Lucy Muir rents a house by the ocean, which turns out to be haunted by a cantankerous seacaptain. Although difficult at first, their friendship blossoms and the captain even 'ghostwrites' an auto-biographical book to bring in money for her. Eventually, the unlikely pair fall in love, only to be challenged when a flesh-and-blood type suitor appears on the scene."

It's London, at the turn of the 20th century. Lucy Muir has been a widow for a year and is living with her late husband Edwin's mother and sister (played by Isobel Elson and Victoria Horne, respectively). Lucy's made a decision to relocate. It's a bold decision because Lucy admits to never having really been on her own, of living a sheltered life. She will move to another location, somewhere by the ocean, accompanied by her daughter, Anna (played by Natalie Wood), and housekeeper, Martha Huggins (played by Edna Best). It's the seaside. . . . "I've always wanted to live by the sea," she says.

Lucy arrives at Whitecliff-by-the-Sea, and despite the resistance of the rental agent, chooses a lovely, somewhat isolated little house called Gull Cottage. We get the sense that this will be her final resting place.

The rental agent resisted Lucy's attempt to select Gull Cottage because, on several occasions previous residents had fled, complaining that the house was haunted. Lucy isn't apprised of this history and indeed rents the house.

As Lucy and the rental agent are walking through the cottage she is palpably and obviously experiencing its perfect fit, its ideal aura, its congruence with her needs. She opens a door and catches a glimpse of a painted portrait of a man in a seafaring outfit hanging on a far wall of the room. The quick exposure to seeing his face in the painting almost gives the impression that the painting is alive—as though it was looking back at her. But as they enter the room, the painting is clearly inanimate. Lucy studies it carefully.

The painting is of Capt. Daniel Gregg (played by Rex Harrison), the deceased former owner of Gull Cottage. Lucy can see the view of the ocean from her sitting room and terrace, and is enthralled with the scenic beauty of it all—except for the monkey tree that interferes with the view and crowds her terrace. Lucy says, "I'll have it chopped down." As she says this, she is suddenly gripped by a strange sensation, as though a disapproving emanation is present in the room. She dismisses this as a momentary passing mood. Later, after cleaning up and organizing the home, Martha, the housekeeper, uses a seaman's expression, saying the room is now "ship-shape."

Everything is building up a sense of a maritime presence; the painting of Capt. Daniel Gregg, the rumor that the house

was haunted, and now Martha's expression of "ship-shape."
In quick order, Lucy shuts and locks the terrace door. An hour
later she is awakened by the same terrace door swinging open
and repeatedly slamming against the wall. It's curious to her
because she was certain she had locked and secured that
door. After a storm the lights go out and she tries to light a
candle but the flame is summarily swooshed out. She tries to
light it again, with the same result. After a moment's pause she
suddenly and with certainty says, "I know you're here. . . . I'm
not afraid of you."

Capt. Gregg authoritatively answers, "Light the candle!" And
now she sees him. "You're Capt. Gregg," she says. They have
a discussion—she speaking nicely, and he, gruffly, and stern-
ly. He's irascible and cantankerous. He reveals that he never
committed suicide but that in his sleep he had knocked over a
gas heater and that's what killed him. He also admits to scar-
ing all the other renters away with his ghostly pranks. But Lucy
disarms him by telling him how much she loves the house.

Lucy seems immune to the issue of a haunted house—this
house.

The Relationship

Gregg basically capitulates to Lucy's charm and sincerity,
not to mention her beauty. It seems that because she's not
afraid of him and actually likes him, a foreshadowing of their
mutual destiny unfolds.

Gregg agrees to permit Lucy to stay in the house—but he
instructs her to move the painting of him into her bedroom.
Moreover, he tells her that he, too, will live in that room. Lucy

is taken aback. After all, she's a decent and proper woman. The Captain's answer to her is that since he is just an illusion, for him to be there is not a real problem. To make logic out of this rather thin argument is somewhat difficult for her but she passively agrees to the arrangement. Then just as he had originally appeared, poof, he's gone.

Suddenly alone, Lucy says: "At least you could have put the lights back on before you left." With that, boom, the lights go on.

At night when Lucy is about to retire, she begins to undress but becomes suddenly self-conscious, and drapes a blanket over the painting. In the course of the next day, Gregg tells her that she's got a good figure and she should never be afraid of it. In other words, he had observed her bedtime preparation. Gregg sees that Lucy has had the monkey tree felled. He is angry about it and they have what might be considered their first lover's quarrel—another indication of their deepening relationship.

During one discussion, the Capt. says that Lucy never really loved Edwin, her late husband. She agrees that Edwin was an "ordinary" man, and then they both agree that Edwin could never have designed "a house like this," the way that Gregg had. Lucy adds: "It's hard to imagine you being ordinary anything."

In due time, Lucy's annuity resulting from Edwin's death runs out. As she will no longer be able to rent the cottage, she is threatened with eviction. However, Capt. Gregg, wants her to stay, he's obviously in love with her. Gregg has an idea. He will dictate a book to Lucy which she will take to a publisher in London, in the hopes that royalties from the book will save the day.

And of course, Capt. Daniel Gregg always knows best.

The Real and the Illusion

They both know they belong together and at one point Lucy, asks him: "What's to become of us?" Gregg tells her that the "us" is not relevant. She's the one who is alive and whatever will be between them depends on what happens to her. At this point in their story, the illusion of their relationship is challenged by what can happen to Lucy in her real corporeal life.

When Lucy takes the finished manuscript to the publisher —a manuscript titled *Blood and Swash*, containing the story of Gregg's's seafaring adventures—the publisher reads it and loves it. At Daniel's instruction, Lucy presents herself as the agent for the author who is away on some adventure —after all, the story is about a sailor's life that takes him on adventures.

And then it happens. At the publisher's office she meets Miles Fairly (played by George Sanders). Miles is instantly smitten with Lucy's beauty and bearing, and manages to insinuate himself into her life. But Capt. Daniel Gregg scoffs at Miles and belittles him to Lucy. Lucy responds by saying: "Daniel, why I believe you're jealous." And of course, Lucy is right, Daniel is very definitely jealous.

Daniel knows that it's only right for Lucy to pursue her real life; otherwise, she would be destined to only have a virtual relationship. Despite his brusque manner, Capt. Daniel Gregg is basically a decent person who would never take unfair advantage, especially with respect to even the most remote exploitation of Lucy.

In Lucy's alternate life with Gregg he had always addressed her as Lucia; now Miles in her real life, simply calls her Lucy. The shift from Lucia in her involvement with an apparition, to Lucy in this possible dawning of a real relationship, is set off by Miles romantically and sensually kissing Lucy—lips to lips. Gregg stands behind a tree and watches. Of course, he knows what this means.

Coincidentally, in referring to Miles, Martha sounds the alarm by saying: "He aint good enough for you." Lucy's answer is: "He's real. . . . I need companionship. . . . I suppose I need love." And, in fact, Lucy indeed, seems to fall in love with Miles. This apparent falling-in-love with a real person is the dividing line separating her illusion from reality. She is now in front-of-the-line, on the reality side.

Gregg knows what it means. He says to her: "You've chosen life." Now, Capt. Daniel Gregg must leave Lucy's consciousness—must leave Lucy to live her life. But before he does, and while she's asleep in her bed, he instructs her to forget all about their relationship, all about his presence, and to believe that it was she that had written *Blood and Swash*. In his watery seafaring language he says with heartfelt regret:

"Goodbye me darling."

The Ultimate Goodbye

Lucy meets with her publisher to review the good news about the success of *Blood and Swash*. Because of this success, she is now independently affluent, and because of this newly acquired affluence, she is able to sign papers enabling her to remain at Gull Cottage indefinitely.

She obtains Miles' address from the publisher's secretary, and decides to surprise him with the news and with a visit. Excitedly, she arrives at his lovely town house and rings the doorbell. A maid answers the door and Lucy identifies herself as Mrs. Muir. As Lucy waits in the drawing room, she notices a painting of a mother and two children hanging on one of the walls. A woman walks in and addresses Lucy as Mrs. Muir and asks innocent questions regarding how Lucy and Miles are acquainted. We quickly realize that the woman is Miles' wife and the children in the painting are theirs. Lucy is obviously mortified. Mrs. Fairley tries to console Lucy by telling her that it wasn't the first time that had happened.

Reality has crushed Lucy again. Of course Martha was right—Miles wasn't fair!

Years pass, and although still quite content at Gull Cottage, Lucy is living a solitary existence. Capt. Daniel Gregg has never again appeared. Lucy's daughter, Anna, is now a young woman who is becoming engaged to be married to a Navy man (another seafaring man), who she brings to Gull Cottage at Whitecliff-by-the-Sea, to meet her mother.

Anna mentions that when she was a child, Capt. Daniel Gregg also talked to her. Anna ascribes his disappearance to the possibility that she got too old and it was no longer necessary to have that kind of relationship with an apparition. She also knew that her mother had the same apparitional experience. Anna then confesses that she thought Lucy had actually fallen in love with him.

Some more time passes and now Lucy is in her later years and she is ill. She dies while sitting in a chair covered with a blanket provided by Martha, who is also very old.

"And now you'll never be tired again," says Capt. Daniel Gregg who has reappeared. "Come Lucia, come my dear."

They are now united in their joint alternate reality. Lucia's younger visage rises like a spirit out of her older corporeal self and they walk together out of Gull Cottage at Whitecliff-by-the-Sea.

Lucy Muir on the Couch

Even before Lucy was planning to live at the ocean, Capt. Daniel Gregg, in his ghostly apparitional state, had been haunting Gull Cottage. He was waiting for her; it was their destiny to be together. Why was Lucy the one he was waiting for?

Lucy was a very sweet, and lovely young woman living in a world that was contaminated with self-serving people, those who were quite content to live the ordinary life. But, she was not like that. In a way, this world was not ready for Lucy Muir, and at the same time, Lucy Muir was made from the stuff of which dreams are made. Of course, dreams are of another domain; they are made in the world of alternate reality. Lucy felt the need to be at the ocean because she intuited she needed a serene place and where she could find peace of mind. Peace of mind always refers to tension-relief.

While we can posit a favorable interpretation of Lucy Muir's decision to withdraw to Gull Cottage for the rest of her life, at the same time, we can see it also as a psychological escape. On the positive side, she is too pure for the world as it was; on the negative side, her withdrawal to Gull Cottage could be a social anxiety symptom that has the derivative effect of forcing Lucy into her ideal dream—her illusory state.

The Meaning of Lucy's Need to Reduce Tension

And now we arrive at the nexus of Lucy's personality that makes the entire story possible—what makes the entire story possible for her. The salient point of Lucy's personality that makes this story psychologically and emotionally possible for her involves her overall need to reduce tension.

In psychoanalytic terms, we are essentially dealing with what Freud postulated as the death-instinct. Without engaging in any interpretation of this so-called death-instinct, suffice it to say that if we boil it down, all the death-instinct really means in this new understanding is that the person wishes their tension to be reduced to zero. In Lucy's case it's a general feeling of not being resonant with the way the world works. She is much more comfortable with a non-peopled nature, by the sea, at Gull Cottage, in Whitecliff.

This is what makes her relationship with a ghost much more familiar than it would be for others who don't share Lucy's need for such solitude; she is actually waiting for death to overtake her, because in death, tension is presumably at absolute zero.

Thus, her dalliance with Miles Fairley was the last straw of disappointments in earthly matters. After that disastrous relationship, Lucy traveled back to behind the line, crossing from the domain of reality to the beautiful rhapsody with a ghost.

It was with the ghost that she felt happiest, and loved, and appreciated. After her experience with the duplicitous Miles Fairley, Lucy migrated further across the line into her alternate reality awaiting her fate, her destiny—to reunite with Capt. Daniel Gregg. Therefore the story created the condition for this woman to see that the only choice for her was to treasure an apparitional relationship, not a tangible one. It is in this sense that *The Ghost and Mrs. Muir* satisfies the criterion of a triangulation of a relationship that ultimately determined her final choice.

Apparently, the Wait Was Worth It

It's a long wait, but when Lucy is reunited with Capt. Gregg, her destiny becomes realized. Gregg calls forth her spirit from her reclined, lifeless corporeal self, to a place where they can forever be together in the absence of any tension whatsoever, in eternal bliss. For Lucy, the wait was worth it.

The ghostly apparitional spirits of Lucy Muir, and Capt. Daniel Gregg, walk out of Gull Cottage together—to an eternity without tension.

Although this particular kind of fantasy/destiny that worked so well in Lucy's favor invites the question as to whether such a thing could ever work for any of us mere mortals, the answer is: Not really.

The moral of the story (the mundane moral), is that in most cases it's probably better to fight it out in the real world rather than to escape into a behind-the-line social withdrawal—even at Gull Cottage, in Whitecliff-by-the-Sea.

Chapter 14

LAURA
(Released, 1944)

A novel by Vera Caspary,
Adapted from her play, "Ring Twice for Lora,"
(Play revised by Vera Caspary and George Sklar)
Screenplay by Jay Dratler / Samuel Hoffenstein /
Elizabeth Reinhardt
Original Music by David Raksin
Produced and Directed by Otto Preminger

Main Cast

Gene Tierney	Laura Hunt
Dana Andrews	Det. Lt. Mark McPherson
Clifton Webb	Waldo Lydecker
Vincent Price	Shelby Carpenter
Judith Anderson	Mrs. Ann Treadwell
Dorothy Adams	Bessie Clary, Laura's Maid

Sample Supporting Cast

Lane Chandler	Detective
Ralph Dunn	Det. Fred Callahan
James Flavin	Det. McEveet
Lee Tung Foo	Waldo's Servant

Introduction

The dramatic device used in this film is the narration of the story by Waldo Lydecker (played by Clifton Webb). In flashback, Lydecker tells his story to Det. Lt. Mark McPherson (played by Dana Andrews) who has been assigned to investigate the murder of Laura Hunt (played by Gene Tierney). But the essence of this film is not the investigation of a murder; it's about how an obsession can take over a person's psyche and turn into a life and death stranglehold.

Typical obsessions leading to endless yearnings usually occur under conditions of unrequited love. But there also exist rather bilious and even macabre obsessions solved only by perverse intention—in this instance, murder. To a person with this kind of pathological, perverse and life-threatening obsession, killing the torturer—the one who doesn't requite the love—seems the only solution.

The Main Story

The DVD describes the story this way:

> ". . . it is the story of a wealthy journalist [who] gets captivated by a gorgeous young career woman named Laura. However, ahead of her

wedding to a dashing playboy, she is found murdered. Stimulated by her portrait, the detective assigned to her case finds that he, too, is oddly under Laura's magic charm."

McPherson and Shelby

Detective McPherson spends a good part of the story in Laura's apartment going through her letters, diary, and other private materials, all the while being kept company by the haunting portrait of her that dominates the room hanging over the fireplace. Her portrait, substituting for her actual presence, seems to consume most of the oxygen of Laura's gracious, comfortable living room. McPherson is definitely under its influence, drawn to Laura's aura, and gradually succumbs to her irresistible looming visage.

Unaware of being taken over by her appeal, McPherson begins falling in love with a ghost, as he plays the musical theme of the film on Laura's phonograph.

In quick succession, McPherson meets the exploitative Shelby Carpenter (played by Vincent Price), who is a parasitic bottom-feeder always trying to insinuate himself into situations that can offer him any possible advantage. He also meets Mrs. Anne Treadwell (played by Judith Anderson), who understands Shelby's exploitative nature very well feeling that water will always find its own level, she believes that her understanding of him means that she and Shelby are meant for each other. Mrs. Treadwell is in a position of power over Shelby who is his fallback support. She subsidizes Shelby whenever he's down and out.

Laura' grew to know Shelby after offering him at a job at her successful advertising firm. Because of the close friendship between Laura and Shelby, Anne Treadwell became quite jealous. Shelby, showing his true colors as a low-life, was carrying on a clandestine affair with another woman, Diane Redford. When Anne Treadwell confessed her love to Shelby, he blatantly rejected her. He had both Diane and Laura to contend with and Anne would add another unnecessary variable to his manipulation menu. Shelby knew Anne would always be there in a pinch, whether or not she ever had him to herself.

Lydecker and Laura

McPherson quickly learns that Waldo Lydecker and Shelby were competitors for Laura's affection, and that although Lydecker had the inside track, Laura seemed to be attracted to Shelby. She and Shelby soon became engaged and Lydecker was enraged. He was madly in love with Laura even though she only treated him in the most platonic manner. Lydecker had introduced Laura to all his high society acquaintances. His position as a high profile journalist and radio personality enabled him to do this.

It was Waldo Lydecker who was chiefly responsible for Laura's success. He relished his powerful position. He gave off an air of cynicism, sarcasm, and a singular superiority but he was also deeply affected by Laura's honesty, absence of guile, her authenticity. With Laura, he could retain his stance of omniscience and yet simultaneously and vicariously experience her warmth and humanity. It was the perfect relationship. Lydecker would be the nasty one, but he would have his good side represented by Laura.

At their initial encounter, he was rude and nasty, but obviously taken with her. He followed up, visited her where she worked, apologized for his behavior, and granted her wish to endorse one of her accounts. The product he agreed to endorse was a pen, and his profile as an accomplished writer made his endorsement valuable.

Their relationship developed with Lydecker supervising everything in Laura's life. They were together each evening for dinner. Laura consulted with him on virtually everything, she was his protégé. Not aware of his personal interest in her and his growing jealously, she began to see other men and would break dinner appointments with him. Lydecker's typical response was to undermine the feelings she might have for any of these men. In this he was quite successful.

Lydecker instinctively, even reflexively, sees that his real major competitor is Lt. McPherson. McPherson, after his prescribed shift, would return to Laura's apartment at night, and have a few drinks. We see that he is now under the Laura-spell. Lydecker accuses him of loving Laura. He learns that McPherson has even put in a bid to purchase Laura's portrait—the portrait that is the embodiment of her beauty and her soul—the portrait that suffuses the room so that you can even smell her. McPherson, sitting there at night in Laura's apartment in a haze and lost in his reverie, barely dozes off when the impossible happens.

In Walks Laura

McPherson is startled out of his reverie and sees Laura standing there as she's entered her apartment. He's astounded, identifies himself, and tells her what has happened. Because she had been away at her country place for the weekend, she had not heard anything of the murder. McPherson realizes it was another woman who had been shot.

Shelby, having become a close friend, had access to Laura's apartment. Knowing she was going to be away, he then had his assignation with Diane in the vacated apartment. Apparently, whoever killed Diane did it thinking she was Laura. If Shelby was the murderer, he had his own reasons for eliminating Diane. The maid, Bessie (played by Dorothy Adams), who adored Laura, walks in and is electrified to see her.

In this phase of the story—after Laura has suddenly appeared—the suspects are Shelby, Anne, Lydecker, and Laura herself. Laura decides not to marry Shelby and naturally, McPherson is happy about that. Anne, who is very astute about such matters, implies that Laura is interested in McPherson. But in a ruse, McPherson arrests Laura for the murder of Diane. McPherson doesn't really suspect Laura but he is setting up a situation where he is slowly smoking out the real killer. The suspects are Shelby, who Laura says "couldn't kill a fly," and Anne, who could and admits she could, and Lydecker, who Laura feels, could indeed kill.

The Clock

McPherson, investigating Laura's apartment discovers that the grandfather clock that Lydecker had given Laura has a secret compartment. He notices that the compartment at the bottom of the clock is large enough to house a weapon. Lo and behold he finds a shotgun in the secret compartment. It now looks as though the murderer was Lydecker. McPherson posts a detective outside of Laura's building and makes sure that Laura's apartment door is locked.

They kiss before McPherson leaves.

Lydecker, lurking outside the apartment door, overhears everything. After Laura turns out the lights and retires to her bedroom, we see that Lydecker has already gained entrance to the apartment. He quietly steps to the clock, removes the shotgun, fills the dual chambers with new shotgun pellets and sets out to kill Laura.

Laura enters the living room and sees him. He's about to shoot her when she pushes the shotgun up toward the ceiling. It goes off, McPherson bursts into the room and Lydecker is shot and killed.

McPherson tells Laura that if Lydecker couldn't have her he was going to make sure that no one would.

Waldo Lydecker On the Couch

With a name like Lydecker, can he really be trusted? The psychological problem with this man is that his needs are precise. They are not fuzzy or confused, they require precise, instant gratification. Because he is not one to be burdened with extraneous problems, he insists, demands, expects, and obtains whatever it is he needs. He has reached a level of adulation for his professional work that enables his every whim to be gratified—and this is exactly what he wants.

In this respect, if his compulsive need is for everything to be precisely ordered, such an aberration will tend to pull him out of his alternate reality and require him to do something quite idiosyncratic in order to make the world conform to exactly how he needs it. Such an alternate reality is defined and characterized as the way in which he has organized everything around him to conform to his exact contours. In a way it is enviable to be in such a position—to have everything fall into order precisely the way you want it. This includes how your household is kept, pristine, with everything in its place, where clutter is entirely absent so that the ambience is quiet—the only sounds you hear are the sounds made by your own making. Lydecker has arranged his life so that he can hear only what he chooses to hear: his typewriter when he's typing, the music he desires, any conversation in which he may be engaged. He can arrange his environment in the exact way he wishes, for maximum beauty and balance—precisely.

In this sense, Lydecker is a man who lives with what is known psychoanalytically as the anal-triad of the need for 'orderliness' (things must be lined-up the way he wants it), 'obstinacy' (nothing happens unless he says so), and 'parsimony' (no clutter, everything in place the way he wants it, and everything done efficiently).

The only problem is that Lydecker needs to be loved, adored, and even libidinized (eroticized) by only one person—Laura Hunt. But he can't quite accomplish this. He almost gets it because she does love him (platonically), and she does adore him (he's endlessly interesting to her and she learns a great deal from him). Laura is not at all interested in him as a man, as a love partner, as a sexual being. In a way, Waldo Lydecker has everything except the second most important thing he would ever want. And this second thing is Laura Hunt.

Of course, the question is: Why is Laura Hunt the second most important thing he wants? The answer is that the first and clearly the most important thing he wants is what he already has: his endless series of precise gratifications—his need for absolute order, neatness, symmetry, discipline, and control over everything on his schedule and in his everyday life. And so, 'control' is the magic word that enables him to have the first thing he wants—his phallic narcissism. Waldo Lydecker adores himself.

Or, does he really?

One would expect that *Laura* is really the story of a solo performer—Lydecker himself. Yet, the larger theme in this movie concerns two major triangles: one among Lydecker, Laura, and Shelby, and the other between Lydecker, Laura, and McPherson. In addition there exist two other triangles associated with Shelby, but these are not as central: one between Shelby, Laura, and Diane, and another between Shelby, Laura, and Ann.

It is clear, therefore, that the movie, *Laura*, is one of *Trios*, and two significant triangles emerge that embrace the entire drama with Lydecker's problems spilling out in both.

What is Lydecker's Need for Such Control?

Lydecker's insistence on order, on control, is actually a matter of his tyrannical need to keep his anxiety at point zero. This is his major wish, and for all intents and purposes, he has achieved it. He always knew that the only way he could achieve this sort of 'control' over his life was not to be entangled in any primary, personal, and persistent love relationship. Yes, he might have friends and acquaintances, but when the day is done, he will never permit these individuals to accompany him home. He knows implicitly that emotional entanglements and true love relationships cannot be controlled in the same way and with the same mastery that he's able to implement as a solo performer. He knows in his bones that when involved with another person one cannot always have his own way. With

Lydecker, not having his way generates a great deal of rage. His need to control this sort of rage, is the reason he has so methodically developed his array of obsessional techniques and narcissistically designed strategies. The point is that such obsessional desire for the control that order and symmetry offer, always keeps anger, and therefore, anxiety, at bay—suppressed, or even entirely repressed.

Hence, Lydecker has kept away from such love entanglements—until Laura. Laura's beauty and sincerity has mesmerized him and has revealed the absence of something deep-down that he knows he needs but which he knows he cannot have. To his dismay, it is not *he* that controls *her*. Rather, it is *she* that controls *him*. In Lydecker's alternate reality of having exactly what he wants, this cannot be permitted. He must take reality and bend it to his will.

Lydecker's Pathology

This is a narcissistically and rigidly obsessional tyranny-of-personality that transcends the normal bounds of the give and take of everyday living. At a certain point of feeling disempowered, such a person can overstep of the norms of normal people. In the absence of concern about typical rules and regulations, he takes things into his own hands. Under such circumstances, this kind of person will be determined not to lose his grip on what he considers to be his prerogatives, as well as his absolute entitlements. These prerogatives and entitlements are personality markers that act to keep his identity in tact.

All of it, the insistences, expectations, willfulness, and need to control produces a psycho-pathological aberration of thinking. It is a pathology that will only permit him to listen to his narcissistic impulses of needing to order the world his way even if such needs and impulses completely ignore what normal people consider to be not just order, but law and order. In other words, in Lydecker's case, he will focus on the order, but ignore the law. The law will mean nothing to him. Civil behavior, civilized law, even civilization itself, will be meaningless to him when such considerations come up against the thwarting of his need for control and consequently the loosening of his underlying volcanic fury—especially, and specifically when he can't have his way.

We can see Lydecker pointing a shotgun in a lady's face and pulling the trigger. When he discovers he killed the wrong person, he goes at it again because he will not tolerate not completely possessing Laura. As long as Laura is alive, he will be tormented that someone else possesses her.

The sick essence of such pathology is that he can actually erase his agony of not having Laura Hunt, only if he 'hunts' her down and kills her. If she's not living, then he's free of his agony and he can again retreat into his circumscribed encapsulated perfect life. If he eliminates her, then he has finally controlled that which threatened the life of his own psyche and thus he will have regained the essential empowerment over all of the variables of his life; since she would no longer be, then he would be free.

Now, comes the problem. If she did love him as a lover loves, then Lydecker would be confronted with an even worse dilemma than he had when she didn't love him that way. Although he would be with her, and possess her, he would need to live in a very untidy situation; he would necessarily need to live with the agony of not always having it his way. He would be in a real relationship without his sky-high need for complete control of all variables. In such a case he would be rendered naked.

Waldo Lydecker surely knows that that's how it would be, and he also knows that in a naked state, he wouldn't look so good.

However, since he would now feel possession of Laura, the idea of killing her would never even enter his consciousness. The net effect of having her would leave him with no option but to suffer; he would have gained Laura, but lost the only Waldo he knew and had ever known, the only Waldo Lydecker he possibly could ever be. He could no longer be the perfect narcissist.

Lydecker was doomed. Without Laura his anxiety is relieved—but in reality he's a murderer, and in the end, he himself is killed. Possessing Laura in a mutual libidinous love relationship would mean that his perfect narcissistic virtuosity would be forever lost—his salient wish in life entirely thwarted. In his own eyes he would become a monumental failure, a person squawking like the rooster of *The Blue Angel*—on his hands and knees!

The Equation Used to Examine Lydecker's Mind

It's a simple examination leading to a useful equation. We start with his wish—his wish is to possess Laura. The wish is thwarted. The 'who' who thwarts his wish to have Laura, is Laura. She is the culprit, and thwarting Lydecker's wish renders him impotent. The principle here is that when his wish is thwarted, a person will always feel disempowered. It is only when a wish is satisfied that one feels empowered. Disempowerment (or helplessness) will always generate anger, and will do so in every person on earth. The reason for this automatic anger response is that when one is disempowered, anger is frequently the only way to feel re-empowered. The point is that anger is always experienced as a re-empowerment. In Lydecker's arsenal of re-empowerments, anger, fury, and rage were his potent re-empowerment weapons.

This simple psychological equation (disappointment of wishes = disempowerment = anger), allows an understanding of Lydecker's need to control everything. Control meant gratification of all of his wishes all of the time. Laura thwarted a most important wish of his—that she should love him and only him. When he couldn't have the wish, he felt disempowered, became enraged, and acted out his reflexive anger by ridding himself of that which made him helpless. He killed her, or thought he did, thus re-empowering himself.

Lydecker heard the instruction of his psyche as being louder and more persuasive than the external voice of reality—and he acted on it. It's what is commonly called "acting-out." Acting-out means "doing something" rather than "knowing something." Lydecker 'did' (killed) rather than 'knew' as he could never tolerate a thwarted wish.

The more general and abstract issue here concerns a mind not understanding itself, or not wanting to understand itself. The question can be asked whether a mind not understanding itself can really, in the truest sense, be called a mind?

And the answer for Waldo Lydecker is that yes, he was highly intelligent, he simply wasn't sufficiently self-aware. He wasn't introspective.

So the moral of the story might be: Remember the commandment—don't do crazy stuff. Rather, know thyself.

Chapter 15

THE BIRDS
(Released, 1963)

From the novelette, *The Birds*, by Daphne du Maurier
Screenplay by Evan Hunter
Music by Mono Mix
Produced and Directed by Alfred Hitchcock

Main Cast

Tippi Hedron	Melanie Daniels
Rod Taylor	Mitch Brenner
Jessica Tandy	Lydia Brenner
Suzanne Pleshette	Annie Hayworth
Veronica Cartwright	Cathy Brenner

Sample Supporting Cast

Ethel Griffies	Mrs. Bundy, Elderly Ornithologist
Charles MacGraw	Fisherman in Diner
Ruth McDevitt	Mrs. MacGruder, Pet Store Clerk
Lonny Chapman	Deke Carter, Diner Owner

Joe Mantell	Traveling Salesman in Diner
Doodles Weaver	Fisherman with Rental Boat
Malcolm Atterbury	Deputy Al Malone
John McGovern	Postal Clerk
Karl Swenson	Drunken Doomsayer in Diner
Richard Deacon	Mitch Brenner's City Neighbor
Elizabeth Wilson	Helen Carter
Doreen Lang	Hysterical Mother in Diner
Alfred Hitchcock	Man Walking Dogs Out of Pet Shop

Introduction

Melanie walks into a relationship not knowing that *The Birds* are waiting! They are organized and aiming to take everyone down.

The movie begins as a puzzle. Birds begin to form aggregates of different species that band together comprising an army with different platoons and even brigades.

In real life, different species of birds never combine or cohabitate like that. Sparrows fly with sparrows, and crows with crows, and never do they join forces. But here, there is some kind of underlying confluence of events, perhaps some underlying force—even perhaps a fiendish, diabolical, and depraved intelligence, one that is villainously focused and with malicious intent. This can be the only explanation for this agglomeration of not merely flocks of birds coming together, but rather, swarms of them. They're all directed toward one goal—that of attacking people—children included.

The Main Story

The DVD describes the story this way:

> "... beautiful blonde Melanie Daniels rolls into Bodega Bay in pursuit of eligible bachelor Mitch Brenner ... she is inexplicably attacked by a seagull. Suddenly thousands of birds are flocking into town, preying on school children and residents in a terrifying series of attacks. Soon Mitch and Melanie are fighting for their lives against a deadly force that can't be explained and can't be stopped ... nature gone berserk."

It's San Francisco. Two people meet in a pet shop. Melanie Daniels (played by Tippi Hedren) is there to buy a mynah bird. Before she enters the shop she looks up at the sky and sees a swarm of birds. Noting this peculiarity, she asks the clerk how many gulls there were.

She meets Mitch Brenner, a lawyer (played by Rod Taylor) who's there to purchase some lovebirds. They engage in a somewhat irritating kind of repartee. Melanie seems annoyed with Mitch who is not really angry, but still has not exactly been a pussy-cat to her. The audience obviously notices her attraction to him; she detects his license plate number and tracks down his address. She buys the lovebirds and sets out on a 60-mile drive to Bodega Bay, a vacation retreat where Mitch lives on weekends with his mother and his little sister. She delivers the birds to his house.

As soon as she arrives in Bodega Bay she spots a sea gull up in the sky. Before that, we see crows in their black silhouette close-ups, ominously flying and screeching.

After Melanie secretly delivers the lovebirds, she makes a dash for it and heads back in a speed boat to the mainland where she had left her car. Mitch spots her and beats her to the punch. When she lands the boat, he's already driven his car around the island, and meets her at the dock. While she was speeding across the bay, a gull dove at her and beaked her on her forehead, drawing blood. Mitch sees it and says to her: "It seems to have swooped down on you deliberately."

Uh Oh, It's Starting.

After patching her up, Mitch invites her to his little sister Cathy's birthday party (played by Veronica Cartwright) and, with a bit of fussing, she accepts. Beforehand, when Melanie had been searching for directions to Mitch's house, she met the schoolteacher in town, Annie Hayworth (played by Suzanne Pleshette). Apparently, Annie has had a past relationship with Mitch which didn't work out, so now they're simply friends. However, it's apparent that Annie still carries a torch for him.

Melanie arrives for dinner at Mitch's house and meets his sister Cathy, and his mother, Lydia (played by Jessica Tandy). Lydia behaves cooly toward Melanie.

Other events begin to unfold, and always in between, we notice that birds are converging. These bird congregations grow increasingly ominous. Greater and greater anticipation is brewing as we wait to see what will happen. Finally, birds start attacking in the middle of town. Gulls attack a gas station attendant and smash into windows, creating destruction, general havoc, and panic. Throughout the movie, attacks are staged both against children and adults.

It's as though something crazy has been loosed!

Why Birds?

Psychologists who specialize in projective-psychology (i.e. critically seeing in others what might really be your own projection—your own problem), find that children will see animals (including birds) in pictures that are vague, much more frequently than do adults. A correlation is drawn between a tendency for a person who sees such images to be an individual with more immature functioning and less control over impulse. It is also theorized that birds can represent underlying hostile impulses, because immature individuals can quickly erupt in anger. In short, the sequence to understanding the symbolic significance of birds here is: immaturity to impulse to anger to birds.

Birds are convenient in a story about random, directed violence of animals toward humans because they are always among us, or above us and there are lots of them. They are also free, they are not confined on leashes, or in cages, or in zoos. Birds are the animals independent of us, unleashed—and, not under our control.

Hitchcock has a delicious sense of mystery and suspense, his feel for the macabre is evident in this film. But the scenes of birds attacking people are not simply eerie, random events. It has meaning, there is a single organizing principle that holds it all together.

What It's All About

No one goes to a psychotherapist to discuss philosophy. Never happens. A patient walks in the door because an event occurred, there was another person involved, and it caused enough anxiety to seek a therapist for some help. What had happened, and who was the other person? It's never a chair or a table—it's a person that is always the cause. The pivotal circumstance will come down to identifying a pivotal person.

This is what we are looking for in our analysis of *The Birds*. We want to know if there is some underlying meaning to all these swarms of birds attacking as an army, no doubt, with a *Commander* at the helm. What is the pivotal event, and who is the pivotal person in the event without whom none of this could have happened? To boil it down, the first question is who is the *Commander*?

Lydia Brenner On the Couch

Yes, it's Lydia Brenner, on the couch. She's the 'who.' And here's how it works.

Lydia is the cause of all the trouble because of her relationship with Melanie Daniels, the pivotal person. All was quiet in Bodega Bay until Melanie arrived. Why? Mitch was nicely living with his mother and Cathy on weekends. Essentially Mitch became a surrogate relationship partner to Lydia, whose husband had died some years earlier. As to Lydia's role in Mitch's life, Annie describes it to Melanie in one word—"Oedipus"—to characterize Lydia's need for Mitch's undivided attention. And the operative term in that sentence is "undivided!"

And that's the key to the entire story. It's the reason the story falls in the category of *Trios*.

What it means is that Lydia is fine if Mitch is hers. But when an oedipal triangle is formed (Mitch, Lydia, and uh, oh, Melanie), this generates tremendous rage in Lydia. With Melanie in the picture, her hold on Mitch is threatened and Lydia's wish to monopolize Mitch will be thwarted if Melanie is successful in corralling him. When Lydia had Mitch all to herself without any threat of a potential rival, it was a tremendous empowerment for her. However, when that wish was threatened or even potentially thwarted, then Lydia (or anyone with a denied wish) felt disempowered. This is the precise reason that the gift to Mitch of the lovebirds set Lydia off. That was the point that the birds began behaving aggressively. It happened even before Melanie arrived on the scene — a harbinger or foreshadowing that something was going to happen to threaten Lydia's relationship with her son.

The hard core psychological and psychoanalytic principle is that disempowerment, without fail, will always generate anger. This is because when one feels threatened and hopelessly disempowered (or actually becomes disempowered), anger/rage is the only thing that reflexively offers the person a sense of re-empowerment. In this case, Lydia was feeling not just angry, but furiously enraged.

Symbolically, it is this rage that gets expressed in the aggression of the birds. The birds represent Lydia's rage at Melanie. It's an oedipal rage. At the end of the movie Melanie is no longer a normally functioning person and can no longer be a viable partner for Mitch. Lydia's rage subsides, and that's when the birds quiet down. Mitch, Melanie, Lydia, Cathy, and the caged lovebirds, can now move unmolested through the ranks of the birds and drive away. To simplify it, when Lydia has accomplished rendering Melanie dysfunctional, she no longer needs to be enraged.

Step By Step

At the beginning—Melanie appears! Though we don't know it yet, her presence itself is a challenge to Lydia. This is immediately reinforced when Mitch enters the pet shop looking for lovebirds—there's no drum roll in the movie at this point but we'll do the drum roll here to underscore and emphasize the point that the first step has occurred.

Melanie heads for Bodega Bay with the lovebirds. This means she's unwittingly closing in on Lydia. But Annie Hayworth confirms it all by talking to Melanie about Lydia, she actually states the case about the oedipal situation as it concerns the inner workings of Lydia's psychology. Without any doubt, Annie understands what Melanie's gift to Mitch means.

And what it means leads us directly to Lydia's anger and to the revealing of the essential definition and description of *the personality of anger*. Here is the definition of the personality of anger:

1. Anger has an aggressive drive. It is inborn.
2. Anger is expansive. It wants to get bigger.
3. Anger has explosive potential. It wants to burst forth.
4. Anger has an attack inclination. It wants to attack.
5. Anger has a confrontational inclination. It wants to get tough.

6. Anger has an entitled frame of mind. It feels it has the right to get tough.
7. Anger sees itself as an empowerment. It eliminates feelings of helplessness or disempowerment.

This is what Lydia is feeling when she sees herself about to lose Mitch to Melanie. She's feeling helpless and disempowered, and such conditions always breed rage. Lydia's fear of losing Mitch disempowered her and therefore, her rage began to quickly gestate.

The birds then, represent Lydia's raging unconscious.

Now we can better understand the meaning of Melanie getting beaked by a diving gull and receiving a bloody head wound as she approaches Mitch and Lydia's house on Bodega Bay at the beginning of the film—actually setting off the chain of events. Mitch mysteriously says: "Looks like the gull swooped down on you deliberately."

You said it, Mitch!

"Deliberately" is the key word here and it's Lydia's deliberateness as well as her deliberation that did it—unconscious though it may have been.

Later, when Lydia met Melanie for the first time she was cold as ice to her. As fate would have it, Mitch invited Melanie for dinner. Then Lydia called a farmer who had sold her feed for her chickens (chickens are birds). She tells him that the chickens won't eat the feed he sold her which is peculiar since chickens always eat anything they can. Lydia claims the feed is spoiled, but the farmer says that he sold another person a different brand of feed and those chickens wouldn't eat either.

Looks like all the birds are acting up and Lydia says: "You don't think they're getting sick, do you?" This is an indirect and unconscious remark about her own 'sickness'—her raging soul. It's her sense that there's something wrong—and of course what's wrong is wrong with her. She even attempts a character assassination by talking to Mitch about Melanie's sordid past. Mitch dismisses it. When Melanie leaves, Mitch spots scores of birds on telephone lines at his house. Apparently, the Lydia army is reconnoitering.

Lydia is obviously the *Commander* of the birds.

At Annie's house, Annie says to Melanie, "Maybe there's nothing between Mitch and any girl because of Lydia." This is when Annie mentions the 'O' word (Oedipus). Suddenly, a gull smashes into Annie's front door. It's as though Lydia is saying: 'You're talking nasty things about me, so here's my warning—Beware!'

At Cathy's party, Mitch takes Melanie up on a ridge with a 360 degree vista of the beautiful outlying topography and the bay of Bodega Bay. It's romantic. They have a conversation that includes a discussion of mother love.

Melanie actually says: "You know what a mother's love is?"

Mitch unabashedly answers: "Yes, I do." Lydia then sees them returning, and she bristles. Immediately thereafter the birds attack en masse. They attack both adults and children. When Mitch asks Melanie to stay overnight, Lydia says: "What's the matter with all the birds?" When Lydia wonders why the birds are behaving this way, it's a quick reference to what is about to happen. Suddenly a swarm of sparrows flies down the chimney and directly into the living room. The fierce swarm represents Lydia's fury that Melanie is staying the night. They all fight for their lives including Lydia who is cowering in a corner of the living room.

This is an interesting psychological understanding of a primary emotion such as anger. Each primary emotion only knows its own instinct; for example fear only knows to flee, and anger only knows to attack. No primary emotion is governed by civilized norms; in this case, for example, anger knows no civilization. It will only direct its energy the way its instinct dictates. In the case of anger, the instinct is to attack, and that's just what Lydia is doing through the birds. The fact that Lydia also is cowering during the attack of the sparrows simply means that the entire thing is a product of her unconscious mind—she truly doesn't consciously know why it's all happening.

By this time her anger is fully unleashed and doing its instinctive mission. When Lydia visits the farmer who sold her the feed and finds him pecked to death with blackened holes for eye sockets (which incidentally, is an oedipal reference in psychological terms). His room is a wreck with windows smashed. In a state of high distress, Lydia drives as fast as she can back to her house. She sees Melanie and Mitch together and for a second or two looks at them with disdain. She runs into the house, pushing through and effectively parting them. It's as though she's saying: 'It's disgusting seeing you both together, all this mayhem is your fault!' It's a moment when she is almost conscious of the absolute fact that their budding romance is the cause of her rage—her rage, in the form of an attacking army of birds.

Uh oh, Lydia knows something. She says: "Do you think Cathy's okay at the school?" She repeats it and then later repeats it again. She even tells Melanie that she wished she understood more, and in the same breath states that she doesn't even know if she likes Melanie. Finally, Melanie goes to the school and notices crowds of crows filling every landing surface. She runs into the school and alerts Annie who is teaching the children a song. They quietly try to usher the children out of the school in order to get them away from the crows. However the crows make a concerted attack on the children who are now screaming and running.

Then at the Bodega Bay diner, Melanie tells everyone that the crows tried to kill the children. A fisherman describes a bird attack on his boat. They all see birds attacking the gas station and hitting the gas station attendant, knocking him down. The gas station area catches fire and turns into an inferno. In a panic, one of the customers shouts at Melanie:

> "They said when you got here the whole thing started. . . . I think you're the cause of all this. . . ."

In a confirming moment, it is Lydia who covers the lovebirds' cage with a large cloth, symbolically eliminating them.

The carnage escalates. When Mitch and Melanie go to the school to pick up Cathy, Annie, is lying sprawled outside on the school steps—pecked to death. So as far as Lydia is concerned, that's one out of the way. It means that Lydia, who was apparently responsible for the failure of the Mitch/Annie relationship, decided in her unconscious rage to finally eliminate any vestige of previous threats. Before Annie was fatally attacked, she rescued Cathy by pushing her into the school.

Lydia is now taking a rest, and a well deserved one at that, after going through all the havoc of expressing so much of her rage. Her extravagant, unrestrained and fulsomely indulged expression of the rage is finally beginning to realize its entire aim. She got rid of Annie—next, Melanie!

Finally, Mitch is boarding up the house; he's nailing shut windows and doors, apparently securing the house in case the birds attack. While he's doing this the birds are gathering. But now, Mitch, Melanie, Cathy, and the caged lovebirds (that symbolically started it all), are imprisoned in the house, apparently, but not actually, safe. Lydia is there as well. It should be noted that when one's rage is so externalized, the person who owns that rage will aim it at targeted subjects but will not harm the self. In Lydia's case, it's clear that her rage is definitely outwardly aimed. It's only when one's rage is internalized (swallowed) that a suicidal implication rather than a homicidal one is raised. Not the case here because Lydia has not swallowed her rage. Rather, she has externalized it and it's obvious that if the birds do gain entry to the house, it's not likely that Lydia or Mitch, not even Cathy, will get hurt.

Guess who?

Lydia now becomes hysterical. She's worried about when the birds might attack and says: "I wish I were a stronger person." Ha. Of course she's worried. She unconsciously knows that the birds will definitely attack, and in force. Thus, in her unconscious life, she's plenty strong. In order for Lydia to eliminate the threat of Mitch abandoning her in favor of Melanie, she knows she needs to finish the job—and she will!

The birds begin their attack feverishly pecking and quite quickly splintering the front door. They crash into one of the windows that had not been completely shuttered. Cathy asks if she can bring the lovebirds into the room and Lydia, in a reflexive moment, shouts: "No!" Cathy says: "Mitch, why are they doing this? Why are they trying to kill people?" At that point, Lydia leaves the room—almost as if fleeing! The birds quiet down and they too, flee.

While Mitch and the others are asleep all over the living room, Melanie is awake and vigilant. She hears something upstairs in one of the bedrooms and goes to investigate. First she glances at the lovebirds sitting calmly together in their bird cage. They're okay. Uh oh, if the Love-Birds are okay then it implies something dreadful might happen to Melanie. Melanie begins climbing the stairs. She slowly opens the door to one of the bedrooms and sees that part of the roof has been pecked and torn away, gulls are sitting at the torn part of the roof looking down into the room. Suddenly a swarm of gulls is on her and she's unable to ward off the attack. She's terribly hurt, bloodied, and dazed, almost unconscious. Mitch appears, fights off the gulls, and drags her out of the room. He shuts the door and gets Melanie down to the living room.

Melanie is now in a fugue state, not knowing where she is. She's in a classic state of shock. But there's a trade-off here. Yes, Melanie is now out of commission, but on the other hand, the birds have suddenly quieted down. The birds are stilled because Melanie is stilled. With Melanie no longer a threat to her, Lydia no longer has any real or essential reason to be enraged. Since Melanie is no longer a functioning person, the mother's rage is naturally attenuated, quieted.

Implicitly, she has her son back.

Mitch insists on getting Melanie to the hospital. He opens the front door and sees that every square inch of ground is occupied by birds. But they are quiet. He steps out of the house and walks carefully and gently, clearing a narrow path through them. He's charting a careful course over to his garage. He drives the car slowly out of the garage to the front of the house. He escorts Melanie out of the house and along with Lydia and Cathy, they all get into the car. Cathy has asked to take the caged lovebirds, and no one objects.

Of course Lydia would never object to getting those love-birds out of her house. Now that Melanie is in a non-functioning state, these birds have lost their symbolic meaning. Now they'll be out of the house.

As they're about to drive off, foreboding lingers in the air. Although the birds are quiet, they could be awaiting some kind of a command from some unknown source. But that's not to be. Mitch drives the car slowly into the distance while the army of birds just sits there in an uncomfortable quietude.

Now that this map of *The Birds* has been presented, what are we left with as the moral of the story? Rather than answer this however, the entire saga begs the question: other than through psychological or introspective investigation, how does one access one's unconscious with consideration to the generally accepted value that it is probably better to know than not know?

When one accepts the possibility that greater introspection can yield access to what is contained in our unconscious mind, birds don't start doing crazy things.

SUMMARY

The psychoanalytic couch is a good place to analyze and uncover meaning that is not easily seen with the naked eye. The psychoanalysis of personality is akin to using an X-ray to appreciate delicate emotional concerns of a person, to see hidden facets of relationships, and generally to better appreciate meanings of behavior.

And that's exactly what we've tried to do in this book. In each movie, we chose a main character to assess. The question is how does one choose that particular character? Should it be a random choice? Is the choice based on the character's stunning looks? Does the character with the greatest deformities determine the choice? Was it the character in the story played by a favored actor so that the choice to analyze that character would seem to be natural?

From a psychological vantage point, none of these above considerations would ever qualify as a factor determining the choice of character to analyze. From the psychoanalytic couch, the character to analyze must be the one most pivotal to the true underlying motive that directs the story in some essential way, or else it is the person most affected by this other pivotal one.

An analogy can be made to a patient who first arrives for a psychoanalytic consultation, and when asked why the patient sought treatment, he might answer: "Well, doctor, I've been depressed all my life." The answer sounds good but it's not specific, and is not at all useful in determining why the person sought treatment, and especially, why now, at this particular time.

The point is that no one consults a psychoanalyst to suddenly want to discuss something that's happened to them "all their life"—unless the thing that's bothered them all their life has recently gotten worse—and for a particular and specific reason. The psychoanalyst knows that people get tense and stressed by other people. Sometimes they get stressed over another person (singular). It was precisely that pivotal other person who created the drama that motivated the phone call for a consultation in the first place.

Such are the linkages that open or introduce any story. There is a pivotal event that revolves around one person, and it is that person who is either the central character of any story, or certainly one of the central characters. It is in this sense that *details need to be specific*.

When we view the film with this particular structure in mind, we see that this essential central character would probably be the most interesting subject for a psychoanalytic analysis. Therefore, the *detail* that becomes *specific* concerns how to identify the pivotal person around whom the story gains its meaning, or in a major way, contributes to its meaning.

Thus, in each of the movies considered here, a theme can be crystallized that encapsulates and becomes a snapshot of what the story is really all about. In the following, this snapshot or summary is presented.

Part 1 — Solos

Part 1, *Solos*: The central character is, of course, the one around which all the action and conflict revolves, this character plays the part of a loner.

Chapter 1, *The Conversation*: This character is Harry Caul. Here, the psychoanalytic issue is a diagnostic one whereby Caul starts out as a guarded encapsulated paranoid person with schizoid tendencies. This means, (as his profession underscores) that he's distant from and suspicious of people, and so Coppola makes him a surveillance expert—essentially, the equivalent of a spy.

Caul's sense that the world is predatory and that one must never trust the absolute nefarious motives of people is simply his own mirror-image unconscious projection. It's not (as he believes) that people are out to get him, the bottomline is that he's out to get them. It's not that no one is to be trusted, it's more that Harry is not to be trusted.

Once Harry has an upsurge of conscience, his guardedness and mistrust are challenged so that in the future Harry will need to put his mastery of the surveillance to better social use.

Chapter 2, *The Day of the Jackal*: The Jackal is a classic diagnostic psychopath without a conscience. He is an assassin whose specialty engages certain elements of voyeurism and stalking. Therefore, he is grandiose and behaves as though he's invisible. He's not at all concerned with rules and regulations. The main psychological point of his motivation concerns his fear of an inner deadened life. This fear of nothing within his inner life other than silence, galvanizes the Jackal to feed on endless external stimulation.

This also means in order to avoid the feeling of a deadened inner life, it becomes necessary to see others dead (or to make them dead) so that he can be relieved that he is not the dead one. The future is bleak for him. He has no choice but to continue to perform high-risk missions for the sake of excitement, or he will die. Fundamentally, his is a case of arrested empathetic development.

Chapter 3, *Predator*: Again, the essence of the story contains the psychological mechanism of projection; at the very root of man's genetic endowment is the premise we are all only interested in the avaricious gratification of our every need. The implication is that if it were not for law and order within civilized society, chaotic behavior would be the norm, and a combination of paranoia, narcissism, and greed would prevail.

The assumption is that even while living in civilized society, residual and strident urges for pleasure lurk beneath the surface. In other words, at bottom, we want it all.

Chapter 4, *Superheroes*: We see that the superhero is a lone player. As children we counted on our superheroes to assuage our anxieties concerning vulnerability, weakness, and essential disempowerment—all of it quite characteristic childhood concerns. In addition, the superhero was completely successful in taming and soundly defeating all the bad guys. This was an oblique reference to the bad impulses that children feel they must conquer if they are to develop successfully and be accepted and loved by their parents and others.

Thus, the superhero is the embodiment of the child's good side defeating the child's presumed bad side. It's good feelings over bad impulses, thereby nullifying all the ostensible badness.

The superhero gives us a chance to breathe more easily.

Chapter 5, *The Passion of the Christ*: The actor/director Mel Gibson himself is on the psychoanalytic couch, and the subject of discussion is the cluster of attack-variations which he portrays in many of his films. In *The Passion of the Christ*, he especially indulges this inclination of linking terrible wrong-doing with a corresponding anticipatory wish for intense, maximum vengeance. Here, these attack-variation themes involve emotions of rage and fury that call for rectification behavior of extreme cruelty. In this way, the motif of relentless vengeance embraced by a raging indignant righteousness is then given legitimate license to be followed by a similar furious corporeal punishment to the identified offender.

Of course, in Mr. Gibson's case, the question becomes whether he is a sole actor in his bias toward "getting even" with the bad guys by fully insisting on an abundance of blood within a fulminating rampaging manic rage? In this sense, is Gibson acting as his father's proxy, set on a singular mission of settling scores, not really an autonomous person with his own individual agenda?

In this proposed fixation of Gibson's that consistently seeks maximum retribution, a question is implied as well as the possible answer—to wit: *Are the sons responsible for the sins of the father, and if so shouldn't the sons be responsible not to repeat the sins of the father?*

Themes of Solos

All in all, the five chapters of Part 1 demonstrate the psychology of individuals who are absolutely determined to create a well defined trajectory for the successful attainment of their aims—aims that are governed by needs for personal

protection, or aggrandizement, or for compensatory gain. Motives of such solo players do not usually concern the welfare
of the other.

The films are an assemblage of movies in which the person
on the psychoanalytic couch is compelled by incessant inner
voices actively lobbying for personal satisfaction, and seeking
safety by insulating and protecting the inner life—frequently
by soundly defeating the other.

The psychological diagnostic issues of this composition
of characters has included: themes that occupy their various
psyches with paranoid and schizoid approaches; the appear-
ance of psychopathic behavior along with a grandiose sense
of being, and attendant over-entitlement; narcissistic preoccupation and its effects; singular ambitious objectives of avaricious self-empowerment; and the use of magical powers that
ensure one's invincibility.

The net effect of such messages leads to the dangers of
insularity and isolation. In this sense, an implicit danger is the
person's need to assuage anxiety. The point is that it's not always a good idea to avoid one's anxiety. Rather, it's probably
more useful to confront one's regressive defenses (that were
used to avoid particularly looking at one's anxiety), and then to
struggle to gain greater maturity. It is with this greater maturity
that we, as social beings, can conquer our fears and hence
engage in more productive social relationships. In this way a
person with greater maturity can accept challenges either to
examine one's own sense of inadequacy or to examine the
need one may have even to avoid looking at personal inad-
equacies (usually accomplished by assuming the stance of
omnipotence).

The bottom line is that introspection can be profoundly useful in contrast to living with an unexamined mind.

Part 2—Duets

In Part 2, *Duets*: The central character on the psychoanalytic couch is one of a couple. It is this character that creates the problem of the coupling relationship.

Chapter 6, *When Harry Met Sally*: It was Harry's attunement to his unfinished business of childhood that prevented him from establishing a bona fide adult relationship. He needed to first fix his childhood so that his psyche could have all unfinished needs perfectly and finally resolved. These needs had the untoward effect of creating a force-field around him that precluded any potential long-term relationship in his adult life.

The problem is that a wish for recreating the past according to how one wants it (and always wanted it), can never be achieved. It usually all boils down to immaturity. What Harry needed to do was to separate from his wish for the perfect childhood, and concentrate on the good-enough adulthood. Thus, it can be said that *the perfect can be the enemy of the good* and for Harry it was precisely this insistence on the 'perfect' that became his enemy.

Fortunately for him, he was successful in defeating his regressive impulse, and could establish an adult relationship with Sally which was quite good enough—actually wonderful. They lived happily ever after.

Chapter 7, *Husbands and Wives*: Woody Allen is on the psychoanalytic couch. The essence of Woody's message is that long-term relationships are far better than being alone, even though such long-term relationships are not perfect. His idea is that personalities of the partners of any relationship are different and such difference will always cause friction. The deciding issue is whether the partners can tolerate the suffering, tensions, and struggle of the relationship rather than immediately throwing in the towel.

Woody knows that the ongoing process of a relationship is far more important than any single episode about which the couple feels disgusted. In this sense, he understands the danger of people living and dying on the basis of each event of the relationship. Therefore, surprise, surprise, Woody opts for a mature view of social bonding which depends really on issues in the relationship being processed rather than always being treated episodically—as final judgment. Sudden judgment of each episodic event by any one of the partners in a relationship is akin to the image of a guillotine ready to be activated at any given moment. In contrast, the processing of any untoward interactions between partners requires give and take and the ability to handle frustration without jumping out of one's skin.

And so Woody's idea is for couples to have a chance for things to unfold and therefore permit the working-out and working-through process to breathe. According to him, hardly anything (or perhaps nothing) needs to be settled by the guillotine.

He's right.

Chapter 8, *The Bridge on the River Kwai*: Obsession and narcissism enables one of the couple, Col. Nicholson, to eventually dominate his counterpart, Col. Saito. It is Nicholson's rigidity and resolute stance that finally supersedes Saito's power and dominance, eventually designating Saito as irrelevant. It was Nicholson's uncompromising and iron-willed stance of self-imposed rectitude that accomplished it all.

The key neurotic factors here are the inherent needs that a person has to express obsessive and narcissistic aims. Although these can frequently help to overcome almost any obstacle in the path of the person's wish, one must be aware of that particular wish because, to put it simply, that wish may actually be a crazy one that could likely take you down, along with everyone around you.

Chapter 9, ***Pretty Woman***: The psychoanalytic drama concerns the gradual transformation of being so terribly stuck in a bad-father transference that Edward Lewis, the high-flying corporate raider, continues to repetitively and compulsively act-out his hostility toward his father by cannibalizing companies, just as he originally did with his father's company. Edward's father had abandoned the family and left it destitute. It was that particular abandonment that buried itself in Edward's psyche.

In his liberation from such an obsessional grip and subsequent compulsive impulse to defeat his father, he meets Vivian Ward, a prostitute who is upright, sincere, and honest, and whose honorable nature begins to soften Edward. However, Edward's true cure arrives in the form of the CEO of a company he's about to capture. This person, a good father image, influences Edward to do the right thing. Edward joins with this man, and in so doing shows he has finally been able to repair what had been almost irreparably damaged—his image of fathers. With the introduction of this good father image, Edward can heal and his acrophobic symptom of fear of heights can recede. He can now, in an uncomplicated way, be on a high place—a partner in a relationship and perhaps a father himself.

Chapter 10, The Way We Were: Katie Morosky was hope-lessly obsessed with Hubbell Gardiner. Her obsession was life-long and it served a hidden purpose. It was this obses-sion with Hubbell that essentially validated Freud's proposition that every symptom is the satisfaction of a disguised wish and that's why we love our symptoms, even if they hurt.

This is how it works: In Katie's case, her Hubbell love-ob-session tortured her, but she wouldn't/couldn't relinquish it even though it was surely also accompanied by anger toward Hubbell—specifically for not requiting her love. As long as she harbored this obsession, it meant that she could keep Hubbell imprisoned in her psyche and in this neurotic and even per-verse manner, keep him forever. So, even though it hurt, she had him.

Here we learn that the psychoanalytic code to freedom from obsessions is to get in touch with your anger toward the per-son of the obsession in order for such a magnificent but tortur-ous obsession to transmogrify into a bird, and fly away.

Themes of Duets

In Part 2, *Duets*, the general message is to try to talk it out with your partner. Love is not enough because people also need to feel understood. In addition, in order to be better able to navigate a relationship, it becomes valuable to try to under-stand one's unconscious motives, and to try and defeat one's obstinate insistence of gratifying childhood needs.

The hopeful message is that change is definitely possible especially if one is aware of the automatic transferences (those voices from the past) that surround all of us in our ongoing relationships.

Part 3—Trios

Part 3, Trios: Relationship conflicts are dramatized by three characters involved in the essential action, one of which becomes the pivotal character on the psychoanalytic couch.

Chapter 11, Casablanca: Ilsa Lund is flanked by Rick Blaine, her former lover, and Victor Laszlo, her husband. Ilsa is torn because she loves Rick, but also feels supremely loyal to Victor. It was Victor who first found Ilsa when she was a teenager. He took her under his wing so that the transference became one of father to daughter. Later on in their relationship Ilsa became very important to him and in fact Victor needed her more than she needed him. In this sense, the original father/daughter transference was transformed into a mother/son one.

The psychoanalytic understanding here is that no matter how much in love a normal woman is with a man, she could never abandon her son for her lover. Therefore, Ilsa ultimately must go with her husband, and forgo the relationship with the man she truly loves. In simple terms, it's the mother's supreme sacrifice for her child.

Chapter 12, The Graduate: Mrs. Robinson is on the psychoanalytic couch because it is she who is the third person in all the implicit oedipal triangular relationships, as well as in the explicit one consisting of herself, Benjamin and her daughter, Elaine.

Mrs. Robinson's oedipal behavior reveals her contempt for her friends, and her husband, along with a distinct 'dissing' of her own daughter. As a result of her dalliance with Benjamin (who is her daughter's age), Mrs. Robinson's behavior actually infantilizes her daughter by dismissing her with the casual assumption of disregard.

Whether Mrs. Robinson likes this interpretation or not, she is in competition with her daughter and all the other women she knows, and this competitive rage is spilling out all over the place.

In the sense of this intergenerational sexual seduction, Mrs. Robinson is seen as instigating an equivalent incest. It is a skewed behavior on her part that also reveals Mrs. Robinson's disdain for her own life's circumstance which, in all likelihood, is the salient variable that has pushed her over the edge. Her sense of a disempowered life has created a repressed anger in her, motivating the necessary feeling that she must acquire power in order to ameliorate this dissatisfaction. Even more importantly, she must wield that power. And does she ever! Benjamin didn't stand a chance.

The Benjamins of the world need to seek a disinterested advisor or, like it or not, they could easily wind up at the Taft Hotel — even though some young men might say that such an assignation might not be such a bad idea.

Chapter 13, The Ghost and Mrs. Muir: Lucy Muir desperately needed to be secluded and away from the everyday din. Lucy's chief objective was to completely erase tension. She meets Capt. Daniel Gregg, a ghost, who inhabits the cottage by the sea that Lucy rents. Of course they fall in love, and this is Lucy's fate — to eventually exist indefinitely in a state of ghostly bliss with the captivating Capt. Daniel Gregg.

Because of Lucy's disappointing experience in real relationships, she opts for an emotional withdrawal from social life and, without a doubt, prefers her solitude. Her experience in her marriage with an ordinary man was not long-lived, and her further experience with another duplicitous man sealed the deal. In the absence of typical everyday tensions of the real world, she will drift off forever into the illusory sunset with her Capt. Gregg. As a psychological maneuver, Lucy's withdrawal is a decision to live behind-the-line inhabiting an alternate reality.

This is a proposed new definition of the death-instinct — bringing tension down to zero. Of course, it would be nice to have a cottage by the sea, yet in real life, nothing is completely or entirely secure, or completely safe.

Tsunamis!

Chapter 14, Laura: The heroine, Laura, is mentored by Waldo Lydecker, a control freak. As an obsessive-compulsive personality with a profoundly narcissistic underlay, his ubiquitous demand is that each and every one of his needs is to be fully gratified. In other words Lydecker will not take "no" for an answer. He needs to nullify all his anxiety so that under it all he can keep his significant anger repressed. In this sense, his is a tyrannical personality concealing an immature belief in all of his assumed prerogatives.

Lydecker is always insinuating himself between Laura and whomever she is seeing. Lydecker can easily be pushed over the edge if the other man is about to win Laura over. And "over the edge" means that Lydecker's grip on reality can be cancelled out under conditions where essentially he can't have his own way — in this case, where he can't control and possess Laura.

It is the case of a man, who because of his extreme pathology has the ultimate choice of either to win, to kill someone (a specifically targeted person), and/or to die.

He does them all.

Instead of achieving all of them, it seems a much better strategy to seek counseling rather than avoid them all; don't always win at any cost, don't hurt anyone, and live!

Chapter 15, The Birds: The story is a simple oedipal one in which a mother, Lydia Brenner, becomes enraged at the possibility of losing her son to a relationship with another woman who will likely marry him. The essence of the mother's rage is represented in the urgent call by the army of murderous birds that are hell-bent on destruction and that actually begin to attack people. These are the Lydia-birds! They are prehistoric, Mesozoic reptilian, with dinosaurian instincts that know no civilization. They just want what they want, period!

The army of birds becomes animated as soon as Melanie Daniels enters the picture and brings with her, a pair of caged lovebirds to Lydia's son, Mitch Brenner.

In the end, the army of birds peck Melanie into a quasi coma-like state, so that Melanie is no longer a sentient person, and therefore, no longer able to conduct a personal relationship with Mitch. Lydia's rage is quieted and the army of birds is, of course, also quieted.

It's the old Greek/Freudian/Shakespearean oedipal dance that begins to quickly shape the story; that is, that Lydia's wish for Mitch to remain with her is an all-consuming wish and will brook no other opinion or option.

This means that Lydia will be furious at Melanie as it is clear to her that Mitch likes Melanie. The symbol of Melanie actually bringing lovebirds into her house is not only an affront to Lydia's basic wish, it's a direct challenge. Therefore, as far as Lydia is concerned, the gauntlet has been thrown!

The validation of the symbolism of attacking birds acting as Lydia's rage-surrogates occurs when the birds have successfully pecked Melanie into a terrified state of shock and rendered her essentially dysfunctional. As Melanie is no longer a candidate for a relationship, the birds behave more like birds and less like marauding killer velociraptors.

Wow, what goes on in a person's unconscious mind is incredible!

Themes of Trios

In Part 3, *Trios*, the basic message is the importance of avoiding participation in love triangles — in relationships where you're one of three. In other words, the message is not to act out, but rather to appreciate the challenge of learning more and more about oneself.

In the psychoanalytic sense, it becomes crucial to make the unconscious material in your psyche more conscious, and more importantly, to try and get in touch with your anger — and especially to try and pinpoint to whom such anger is directed. A primary emotion such as anger will always be directed to another targeted person.

Conclusion

In all three parts of this book, every character's wish in every film was the root of all problems. That the wish is blocked or thwarted by an outside source (another person), is the fount out of which all subsequent story action and behavior is derived. It's clear that this failure to have the wish realized creates the problem that sets off any conflict; it sets off the problem that animates the story.

The main point here is to ascertain the character's wish, and then assess to what extent the wish was or was not gratified.

It will thus enable one to understand the underlying motive in that pivotal character's general behavior or nefarious or neurotic activity.

One thing is for sure: stories will always contain an underlying drama clothed by the descriptive plot line so that without an understanding of the story's latent content, one will come out of the theatre thinking: "Well, leave it to Hitchcock to give us a great movie, but birds could never do that!"

And that's why a deeper understanding will enable one to become the analyst that puts *Hollywood Movies on the Couch.*